Praise for *Never Coach on an Empty Stom*

"Richard makes people wake up. His coaching framework brings alive the best possibilities in both you as a manager and the individuals and groups you lead. From the first coaching engagement fifteen years ago, Richard has become a friend and trusted advisor. This is a must-read book for every leader (early, mid, or late in career) who wants to engender respect, engagement, and results from direct reports."

—Bob Wolpert, Corporate Senior Vice President of Golden State Foods, and President, Quality Custom Distribution (QCD)

"The simple and practical ideas in this book will forever change how you manage."

—Renee Bergeron, Senior Vice President, Global Cloud Channel, Ingram Micro Inc.

"The richly detailed storytelling and careful analysis turns this book into a page-turner I did not want to put down. This is clearly the right message told in the right way to all managers seeking ways to help create a high-performance culture from their management, and coaching skills. The correct coaching methods that Greenberg is able to demonstrate are the keys to great leadership."

—Keith Oldridge, former CEO and Vice Chairman, Swann

"This book is a must-read for anyone who strives to sharpen their skills in leadership, management, and creating a powerfully productive organizational culture. Richard Greenberg has written the ultimate coaching guide for leaders at all levels."

—Judy Belk, President and CEO of The California Wellness Foundation

"As I read this book the smile on my face became brighter, larger, and more joyful with each chapter that I consumed. This is a peaceful and easy read, bursting with equal parts wisdom and practicality. I am quite sure this book will become my newest companion, guiding me step-by-step on my journey to find that elusive balance between work and play."

—Nancy Pope, Senior Vice President, Paramount Pictures

"A wonderful book for every manager who wants to improve their coaching skills. Richard Greenberg is incredibly wise, and this insightful book is like having the benefit of a one-on-one conversation with him."

—Caryn E. Angelson, Executive Vice President, Chief Human Resources & Chief Legal Officer, TMNA Services, LLC

"The definitive book for every manager who wants to improve their coaching skills. A jargon-free read that offers clear and practical steps any manager—rookie or veteran—can apply with their teams to improve results. I give this insightful book my highest recommendation."

—Tom Norton, Senior Vice President Human Resources, KB Home

"This book offers managers the skills and confidence to navigate the tricky waters of coaching. It provides the wisdom and insight that will help any leader and manager dramatically raise the performance level of individuals and teams."

—Chris Stehman, HR General Manager at Yamaha Motor Corporation, U.S.A.

"Richard Greenberg understands how to unlock the potential and full energy of our leaders. He has been coaching executives and managers for the past twenty years plus, and now this book is his generous 'how to' for all. He shares the practical steps we can take in developing our teams. Wonderfully engaging and great stories that capture why developing others is a competitive capability, but more important a self-reflection journey—that matters deeply to who we are authentically. Read this book, and buy one for each of your team members."

—Sherry Benjamins, Founder and CEO, S. Benjamins & Company

"An indispensable guide with a practical and easy-to-follow framework for all managers to find their unique path to high performance for their teams and their organizations."

—Roger D. Lambath, AVP Transportation–Northern Region, Union Pacific

"This exceptional book describes in clear, basic language how competitive advantage can be gained through managing and coaching. Richard's simple recommendation to coach yourself as well as your team provides a roadmap that a manager in any field can follow. In Richard's words, 'The greatest coach in the world cannot help someone if they don't want to help themselves.' His advice to 'begin again' and 'help someone see possibilities for improvement' has over the last several years helped increase my own team's efficiency and ability to remain focused on continuous improvement."

—Tracy Burdine, Director Client Services, Yusen Terminals LLC

"Richard Greenberg brings to life your responsibility to manage yourself first, and then use proven coaching techniques, to set your team on a course toward success. His wisdom and insights, gained from guiding countless workplace leaders, will revitalize your leadership skills."

—Mike Deblieux, SHRM-SCP, Principal Consultant, Deblieux LLC

"Richard opens the lines of communication between yourself and your direct reports with easy-to-remember tools that provide immediate feedback. Developing the people who work for you is the most important thing you can do as a leader, and this book gives you the tools necessary to do so."

—Sean Marron, Director of Operations, Yusen Terminals LLC

"I love Richard Greenberg's fresh and holistic approach to the critical topic of coaching. *Never Coach on an Empty Stomach* offers in-the-trenches, actionable tools, templates, and tactics that will help managers elevate their impact—and the impact of those whom they lead."

—Julie Winkle Giulioni, co-author of the bestseller
Help Them Grow or Watch Them Go

Richard Greenberg has a well-honed view and demonstrated commitment to developing, enhancing and maintaining long-term, positive, and productive relationships, coupled with a broad understanding of what it takes to succeed as a leader in today's complex world. This book will revitalize and maximize your leadership and mentoring skills.

—*Richard Goren, D.D.S., Chief Dental Officer, LIBERTY Dental Plan*

"Richard is an extraordinary executive coach with whom I've worked for many years. We share a belief that coaching can be transformative in terms of personal insight, confidence, and results-driven performance. His book is a consolidated guide for any manager to begin their journey into coaching, for themselves and their team members."

—Mary Herrmann, Managing Director, Executive Coaching, BPI group

NEVER
COACH
ON AN
EMPTY
STOMACH

**Bite-size Actions
to Energize People and Teams**

RICHARD A. GREENBERG

405
NORTH
PUBLISHING

ISBN 978-0-9994890-0-0 (print)
ISBN 978-0-9994890-1-7 (e-book)

405
NORTH
PUBLISHING

4712 Admiralty Way, Suite 518
Marina del Rey, CA 90292

DEDICATION

*To my wife, Renée, for the bliss we enjoy and the challenges we endure.
Here's to more of both in the years ahead.*

*To my children, Robert and Rachel, for the overwhelming
feeling of gratitude I feel every day because of you.*

*To my father, an author and teacher and, most meaningful to me:
the Best Dad in the World.*

*To the memory of my mom, the most brilliant and
kindest person I have ever known.*

*To my sister and brother-in-law, who continue to show
me what love and strength really are.*

CONTENTS

FOREWORD

I cringed when I first received this book.

Richard Greenberg has been both a dear friend and valuable working partner of mine for many years and eagerly asked that I read it. I knew that he had been working on it for a long time and was very pleased with the result. What if it was awful, or even just mediocre? How was that conversation going to go? What's worse, he asked if I would write the foreword. What would I say? "There are many books about coaching, and this is one of them."

Fortunately, my fears were baseless. This book is flat-out terrific. But enough about me. What does this mean for you? Why another coaching book?

Because: this book contains a lot of new information translated into a proprietary process and driven by an original point of view. There is great depth here, yet the book is easily accessible. Every strategy is backed by a practical, tactical plan. Every business case for application is supported by the personal motivation to apply it. Richard isn't simply writing here; he is—no surprise—coaching you through how to gain or increase this essential skill. Like only the very best business books, *Never Coach on an Empty Stomach* brings science to the art of management, and art to the science of creating business impact.

There are plenty of smart books about coaching, but few wise ones, since wisdom comes from experience applied to intelligence. Many business authors

NEVER COACH ON AN EMPTY STOMACH

have scant history of applying what they preach to others; they just think it's a good idea. Richard has regularly created success for his many coaching clients through the application of what he now reveals to you. His good ideas produce results.

This is a business book that is also a delightful read—warm, intimate, and fascinating. It's because Richard is exactly the same guy in life as he is in these pages. He is quietly confident in his abilities, reliable in his promises, and ferocious in his commitment to those he chooses to serve. He chooses to serve you in this book, and every page, every recommendation, and every tactic is offered to you with that in mind.

But enough about you. Back to me for a minute. I am an author myself and also own an international consulting company. This puts me in constant contact with managers all over the world. What I've seen in the best of them, from executive to entry-level, is that they take coaching others seriously, as a source both of their own immediate success and their legacy impact. They also tend to coach themselves using the same principles.

Are you a manager by profession and interested in getting better at it? Or do you want to become one for the first time? Are you a coach by profession and interested in getting better at it? Or do you want to become one for the first time? If the answer to any of these questions is yes, then this is a book you must read.

One more thing: After reading this book myself, I now realize that Richard has been slyly coaching me all these years. Like so many others, I owe success to Richard Greenberg.

Stan Slap

New York Times bestselling author of

Bury My Heart at Conference Room B and *Under the Hood*

[**I**]

INTRODUCTION

Why are some managers consistently capable of driving great results for their organizations and their teams? Why are the people and teams that report to these managers invigorated and energized by their work? Do these successful managers share a secret that allows them to succeed within different challenging environments, in different industries, and with different teams? They do—and any manager who wants to help build a trustworthy and highly successful organization might profitably take it to heart.

Remember this: The most profound skill you can learn and practice on a regular basis is helping the people you lead participate in work that is meaningful…to them. Making progress toward something personally meaningful produces the best condition for motivation.

Self-interest is a strong motivator. When your team members believe their needs can be best satisfied by their work experiences, they will dedicate time and energy to achieve goals for you, their team, and the organization that makes it possible to fulfill those needs. This positive energy translates into higher work performance.

Here's a brief story:

Several years ago I was hired by a long-term client to facilitate a merger between their company and a competitor of roughly equal size. Both companies had similar revenues, and each had about 40,000 associates. Profitability was a different story, but the integration was generally referred to by the financial press, customers, and investors as a legitimate "merger of equals." While I believe there is no such thing as a true merger—they are all acquisitions in my view—this one was about as close as you could come to an integration of very similar companies, functioning in the same industry and under the same operating conditions. Still, there was no arguing that my client was the acquirer and its president would come out on top as the CEO and chairman of the board of the integrated company.

The planning work for the merger was done in a large project room, with about fifty members of the acquiring firm, outside counsel, and consultants. The room was festooned with graphs, organization charts, action plans, and about a dozen easels with flip charts. It was loud, and it operated 24/7.

About four weeks into the assignment, the president and the CFO of the acquiring company burst into the room, each holding a bottle of champagne in both hands, big smiles on their faces. "Stop everything you're doing," shouted the president. "We are not going through with the planned merger. In fact, we are going to be acquired by…." (He named another big player in the industry.) The big, loud room went silent.

As the last molecule of air was being sucked out into the hallway, the president gently placed the champagne bottles on the table. He spoke in a soft voice: "What I just said is not true. We are going ahead with this merger as planned. You are all important to the success of this action. I know you know that. But I wanted you to feel something. I want you to emotionally connect with what people in the other company are going through. Think of their needs and interests. They are worried, and they are fearful. And, just like you less than a minute ago, they are wondering: 'What's going to happen to me?' But, unlike you, they are still asking that question. We have to have an answer for them in a timely and honest manner. If you are not working on that question, let's start now."

I talked with the president later and told him he had made the greatest demonstration of symbolic leadership I had ever seen. His simple reply: "Leadership? No. That was 100 percent coaching. I needed to jolt them into a state of empathy, into a new way of thinking. I wanted to remind them of the power of self-interest, so they would focus on what people at the other company want most now—such as security; certainty; and consistent, clear, honest communication. Let's focus on what they care about first. Then maybe, just maybe, they will be more energized to work with us, and this integration will be a lot smoother."

Find a quiet spot. *Open your mind* as you read this book. You are going to explore why you can't remain a good manager, or become a legendary one to your company, customers, and teams, without also becoming a better coach. And you are going to take the small, steady, and important steps to get better at coaching.

ROADMAP

Never Coach on an Empty Stomach combines a proven coaching framework with a practical guide to applying and adjusting the framework to fit your business and personal life—one step at a time. This is an *open-source* coaching menu, available to all who want to use it.

This book is about helping you successfully cross the threshold from being a good manager to being a great manager with a reputation for achieving sustained positive value to your company and positive energy for your teams. You can achieve this by steadily and systematically improving your coaching abilities. Consistent improvement is possible by climbing five rungs of disciplined action that comprise what I call the *Coaching Ladder to High Performance*. I have coached hundreds of managers and leaders across the globe using this methodology—an approach combining equal parts structure and flexibility. The tricky part is understanding not just the mechanics of *what* to do, but *how* to get it done.

This book explains what to do and, more importantly, focuses on how to successfully practice each discipline, using case studies, coaching stories, and

COACHING LADDER TO HIGH PERFORMANCE

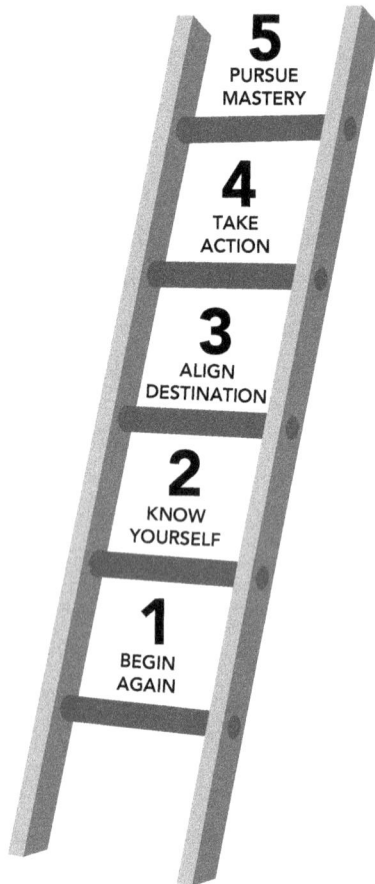

5
PURSUE
MASTERY

4
TAKE
ACTION

3
ALIGN
DESTINATION

2
KNOW
YOURSELF

1
BEGIN
AGAIN

business examples. As a manager myself, I know how much time you devote to your organization and your team. You likely spend 70-plus hours a week thinking about work, traveling for work, and actually doing the work. I also know you want to help build and grow your organization and you want to make forward progress—not completely defined by your organization's terms, but on your terms too. This book will show you how improving your coaching skills helps you and your team align with your organization's strategies and achieve your goals for success and fulfillment.

- » Discipline 1: Begin Again
- » Discipline 2: Know Yourself
- » Discipline 3: Align Destination
- » Discipline 4: Take Action
- » Discipline 5: Pursue Mastery

To produce the desired results, the ladder's Five Disciplines should be pursued in sequential order. By climbing the ladder of rungs one disciplined action at a time, you experience the advice and guidance offered at each stage, with each action building on the previous one. Once you've reached the top of the ladder, the disciplines can be revisited as needed to help you coach others in pursuing and accomplishing their goals. Or simply revisit the *Discipline Summary* or *Energizers* sections at the end of each chapter for encouragement and ideas.

This book will give you a series of practical and straightforward steps to improve many of the skills you already have but don't use often enough. This is not a "transformation" of what you do or a "re-engineering" of you as a manager. I am not asking you to give up the manager, director, or VP title you have earned. I'm inviting you to enhance your role by activating and improving specific coaching skills, positively impacting the people you manage, and achieving greater results for your team and your organization.

Be aware, however: While coaching is easy to learn, it can be difficult to sustain. This book is designed to help you improve, practice, *and* sustain your coaching skills.

THE BUSINESS CASE FOR IMPROVING YOUR COACHING SKILLS

The Middle English word *coche* originated in 1556 to refer to a particular kind of carriage, a means of transportation. The original purpose of the *coach* is to help someone move from where they *are* to where they *want* to be! The most effective coaches help people see beyond what they are today to what they can become tomorrow.

I can tell when someone has worked effectively with a manager who has mastered both *what* to do as a coach and *how* to coach. Here are the differences I have noticed:

The person *without* a positive coaching experience with their manager...	The person *with* a positive coaching experience with their manager...
Less knowledgeable about who they are and less clarity and confidence about where they want to go	More introspective, more aware of their personal core values and how to fulfill them
Fragmented focus or laser focus on low-priority tasks	Clear thinking about what is urgent and important; an ability to prioritize
Defensive low-energy behaviors driven by self-interest and/or self-doubt	Heightened energetic concern for the welfare and benefit of the team, organization, and peers

WHY MANAGE *AND* COACH?

You do your job as a manager, and you do it well. As a "working manager" you may even do everyone else's job. And now you are going to add "coach" to your list of responsibilities? Before you close this book, muttering, "I don't think so," read on a bit more and then decide. I know you are busy and you work hard. I know you already devote a lot of energy and time to figuring out how to motivate teams and individuals. But I also know that improving your coaching skills will not only make your role as manager easier and less stressful, it will also help your organization achieve significant and sustainable competitive advantages.

And you will not have to abandon or ignore what your organization most wants from you: ferocious energy, fanatical loyalty, fierce protection of organizational assets, innovative problem solving, hunger for enterprise growth and new opportunities. Improving your coaching skills helps you use all of these traits more effectively.

When done with the right combination of structure and flexibility, your coaching will unlock doors that often remain closed to struggling, off-track teams and individuals—as well as high-flying, high-potential ones. No manager working today is ever 100 percent immune to becoming, as author and colleague Dr. Bruce Heller puts it, "too painful to keep and too valuable to fire." Adding to or improving your coaching skills can often change this dynamic and instill a perception in your boss and peers that you are, in fact, too valuable to lose.

You can be the type of coach who will increase individual and team energy, emotional commitment, and engagement. The need to expand and improve your coaching skills for the people who report to you has never been greater.

The demands on managers today to deliver results—profitability, growth, quality, market share, productivity—have never been more stress-inducing. You are managing in an age in which

» Cloud-based computing, mobile devices, and other applications support remote, independent workers.
» Multiple generations in the workplace have different, sometimes competing, demands and desires.
» Incentives must be more than monetary.
» Technology drives innovation at a lightning pace.
» The demand for top-tier talent has never been greater.

How do managers stay on top of these challenges? The traditional employee-manager relationship is undergoing seismic shifts, and the leader who can coach at just the right moments will be in demand by organizations and teams. Done right, they will achieve great results for their companies and teams.

I didn't write this book because it's nice to be a coach or because the subject interests me. I wrote it because, in this environment and the one that is coming—a defining age marking new and interconnected relationships between intelligent managers and team members, and artificially intelligent machines—it's urgent for managers to improve their coaching skills.

The work world is largely influenced by whom you report to: your direct manager. If your organization is letting you down but you have an energizing manager, odds are you will feel good about your work and expend energy and effort to help your team. On the other hand, if you work for a best-in-class, highly-admired company but you report to a poor excuse for a manager, it becomes very hard to do your best work and feel good about it. The old adage is true: we work for people, not organizations.

When managing *and* coaching become an everyday way of thinking and working, you will experience more focus, freedom, and fun at work, and so will the people who report to you. Managers who coach help provide fuel for people and teams to produce business results that are both quantifiable and qualitative. The formula is not rocket science:

$$E = MC^2$$
$$E = Energy$$
$$M = Managing$$
$$C = Coaching$$

To achieve the maximum energy potential of the people reporting you, every minute of managing should be complimented with two minutes of coaching. This book shows you how to do this.

Coaching Produces Tangible, Bottom-line Performance Results

The use of a coaching scorecard measures return on the time invested in your coaching. The scorecard is explained in *Discipline 3: Align Destination.* The chart below displays some of the quantitative metrics and scorecard comments I have seen when managers apply the framework, tools, and tactics described in this book and then link their coaching to the creation of a high-performance culture.

Metric	Coaching Scorecard Comments
Market Share	"Increased market share by 4% without sacrificing margin."
Q1 on-time deliveries	"Q1 deliveries goal exceeded by 22%."
Q1 sales-plan targets	"Q1 sales plan for pretax income exceeded by 14%."
CSI (customer satisfaction index) score	"Customer satisfaction index score has improved by 3%."
Q3 customer commitments	"Q3 to date: 100% of commitments met and 'on time.'"
Top-line revenue target	"Top-line revenue exceeded annual forecast by 16%."
Sales productivity	"10% year-over-year improvement for business units in North America, Latin America, and Europe in sales productivity."
On-time delivery	"Year 1: Routes 150, deliveries 596, clean invoice 88%, fill rate 99.82%, on time 93.12%. Year 2: Routes 169, deliveries 692, clean invoice 94%, fill rate 99.96%, on time 98.25%."

Coaching Allows Unique and Better Ideas to Surface

Coaching encourages sharing of ideas and different perspectives. People can get fixated on their own points of view and waste time trying to convince others of their opinions. Managers who steadily improve their coaching skills understand that the true spirit of innovation and improvement consists of building on many points of view to bring multiple ideas and perspectives out into the open.

> *"If you have an apple and I have an apple and we exchange these apples, then you and I will still have one apple. But if you have an idea and I have an idea and we exchange these ideas, then each of us will have two ideas."*
>
> —George Bernard Shaw

Coaching Opens the Door to a Second Chance to Make a First Impression...For Anyone and Everyone

It's possible to recover from a terrible first impression, but it can take significant time and a series of highly advanced nuanced skills. A better way to correct a bad first impression is with coaching. At the beginning of each new coaching assignment, I explain the "coaching honeymoon." This is a period of time when key stakeholders to the person being coached (e.g., the boss, peers, direct and indirect reports) understand the coaching process is in a very early stage and they become hyperaware of any changes they perceive in the person's behavior. In essence, the individual being coached has a second chance to make a first impression with people they work with—a new and more positive impression about their personal and professional brand.

The key stakeholders are watching, waiting, and eager to perceive something different and better. The same phenomenon will happen when you coach teams or individuals after reading and applying the steps in this book: they will recognize, as you also will, that your coaching is providing an opportunity to put aside past opinions and biases and is opening that door to a new "first impression."

This book gives you a second chance to make a first impression. The steps for how to improve your coaching skills are easy to follow and implement. When you practice them, people will notice the difference. Your brand as a manager will be enhanced.

Coaching Encourages Vulnerability

The best managers and leaders I have worked with live by Rick Warren's principle: "True humility is not thinking less of yourself; it is thinking of yourself less." We often must surrender certainty and the need to be right in order to be trustworthy to others. People who have worked with a manager who coaches are more open and authentic with themselves and with others in ways that allow for renewal, as well as for personal and professional growth.

Coaching Challenges the Status Quo and Established Mindsets

Coaching managers help people break out and break through into new ways of thinking and seeing, by helping them ask challenging questions—the ones that often begin with "why?" or "why not?"

There is another, more fundamental reason for you to read and apply this book's tools and principles. To quote Mahatma Gandhi: "If we could change ourselves, the tendencies in the world would also change." The world's quintessential coach is saying that personal and social metamorphoses go hand in hand. As a manager, you can better fulfill your coaching obligations to *others* if you first make a solo climb of each rung of the high performance ladder yourself. Gandhi knew this well, as this classic story illustrates.

During the 1930s, a young boy became obsessed with eating sugar. His mother was upset about this, but no matter how much she scolded him and tried to break the habit, he continued to eat sweets. Frustrated, she took her son to see his idol, Mahatma Gandhi. Perhaps, she thought, her son would listen to him.

As the story goes, they walked for many hours under a scorching sun to reach the Mahatma's ashram. There, she shared her concern with Gandhi: "Bapu, my son eats too much sugar. It is not good for his health. Would you please advise him to stop eating it?"

Gandhi listened to the woman carefully, thought for a while, and replied, "Please come back after two weeks, and I will then talk to your son."

The woman, confused, wondered why Gandhi did not ask her son to stop eating sugar right away. Nonetheless, she took the boy by the hand and led him away.

Two weeks later, they visited Gandhi again. Gandhi looked directly at the boy and said, "Boy, you should stop eating sugar. It is not good for your health."

The boy nodded and promised his idol he would not continue this bad habit any longer. The boy's mother was again confused. She turned to Gandhi and asked, "Bapu, why didn't you tell him that two weeks ago, when I first brought him here to see you?"

Gandhi smiled. "Two weeks ago, I was eating a lot of sugar myself."

This book will not ask you to coach others—until you experience some coaching advice yourself. You can begin by reading it and practicing what it recommends. Once you've done so, you will be prepared to coach others to achieve their professional and personal goals. You will be free of the sugary-sweet and ineffective managing and coaching habits that, in the long run, deplete your energy and the energy of your team members.

DISCIPLINE 1:
BEGIN AGAIN

"I have approximate answers and possible beliefs and different degrees of certainty about different things, but I am not absolutely sure of anything."
—Richard Feynman

"The word 'listen' contains the same letters as the word 'silent.'"
—Alfred Brendel

"So, little by little, time brings out each several thing into view, and reason raises it up into the shores of light."
—Lucretius

The "coaching" provided by managers too often moves in the opposite direction of that noted by Lucretius in the quote above. With the hectic pace that dominates the working day, it's understandable for a manager, reflexively scratching the itch of the urgent, to miss a breakthrough coaching moment. Many managers—not you—don't think they have time, in their high-pressure environments, to pause, coach, and help people grow.

Sometimes, if you have felt the bite of the perfectionist bug, it's easier just to finish the work yourself. If you start to hear the siren song "Good Enough," you might allow delivery of subpar products and services, believing that this only minutely detracts from quality goals and standards.

Managers can and must act on the unusual, take hold of a coaching moment, and bring a development opportunity *up into the shores of light.* This is what coaching offers, after all: the ability to slow down time, if only for a brief moment, to zero in on the vital learning that can occur in the smallest things. This is why coaching matters and will always matter: it recognizes and creates time to focus on opportunities for people to do better—for themselves, their teams, and their organizations—and, more importantly, to *be* better.

BEGINNER'S MIND

The first discipline in the Coaching Ladder is to Begin Again—to help someone see possibilities for improvement. The manager, after all, is only going to be effective if the person being managed has a "beginner's mind," a willingness to learn and trust.

Shoshin is a Zen Buddhist concept meaning "beginner's mind." It refers to having an attitude of openness and a lack of preconceptions when studying a subject, even at an advanced level, just as a beginner would. The value of this is best summed up by Zen Master Shunryu Suzuki: "In the beginner's mind there are many possibilities, but in the expert's mind there are few."

No one learns who doesn't want to learn. No one improves who is not willing to stumble. No one alters their behavior if they don't want to change. The greatest coach in the world cannot help someone if they don't want to help themselves.

In organizational life, policies, procedures, processes, and performance systems don't exactly seed and cultivate a beginner's mind. They recognize and reward an experienced mind—a mind that "fits in" and sets the body in motion to act in predictable, safe, and sanctioned ways.

I have found that letting go of self-centeredness—for the coach and the coached—is an entry point to the beginner's mind. Someone with a beginner's mind realizes they don't always have to be the star of their own movie. They can be the producer. They can be the director.

SIX KEY TRAITS OF THE BEGINNER'S MIND

1. OBSERVANT NATURE

GENERAL DESCRIPTION: You are an impartial witness to your own and others' experiences. You possess a self-detecting awareness about your tendency to categorize experiences as good or bad, and you avoid these judgments as often as possible. When you coach, you don't predetermine. You see, hear, listen, ask, and share, with a constant focus on improvement.

HOW IT MAY LOOK: A person with a beginner's mind is vigorously involved in the neutral act of observation. The nonjudger takes in information before rendering an opinion regarding the value or merit of what is being observed. Effective coaching managers don't judge people; they share ideas and opinions about behaviors and actions. There is an old expression: "Judging someone does not define who *they* are; it defines who *you* are."

2. PATIENCE

GENERAL DESCRIPTION: You realize that activities require time, incubation, discovery, and reflection, and that non-urgent activities should never be rushed. You have an in-depth understanding that quality work requires time. You are patient and wise enough to balance the time needed to succeed with the external pressure to complete the activity as quickly as possible.

HOW IT MAY LOOK: Patience moves our minds away from frustrations, expectations, or "shoulds" and aligns us with reality. It can look and feel like calm confidence and strength in the face of conflict and provocation. Being patient does not mean we must just "take it" if someone is abusive or creates problems. There is a time when it is okay to tell others if and how their actions or conduct are hurtful or disrespectful.

Leonardo da Vinci is credited with saying, "Patience serves as protection against wrongs as clothes do against cold. For if you put on more clothes as the cold increases, it will have no power to hurt you. So, in like manner you must grow in patience when you meet with great wrongs, and they will then be powerless to vex your mind."

3. SENSE OF HUMOR

GENERAL DESCRIPTION: You don't take yourself too seriously, yet you know the importance of serious work and the connection between having fun and achieving great results. You are able to let go of your self-induced illusions of "knowing" in order to be present and open to true experience. You also know this can make for some pretty embarrassing mistakes. That's OK! Not only does most of your real learning come from mistakes, but your most embarrassing mistakes make for great humor.

HOW IT MAY LOOK: Humor tends to have an edge to it, so at work people typically tone it down or avoid it altogether. It's hard to do well and easy to do badly, especially because of the tendency to take ourselves too seriously. But a Robert Half International survey, for instance, found that 91 percent of executives believe a sense of humor is important for career advancement. Another study by Bell Leadership Institute found that the two most desirable traits in leaders were a strong work ethic and a good sense of humor. At an organizational level, Zappos and Southwest Airlines use humor to brand their business.

Well-placed humor that is clever and appropriate to a business situation enhances your status as a leader, manager, and coach.

*"A sense of humor is part of the art of leadership,
of getting along with people, of getting things done."*
—Dwight D. Eisenhower

4. HUMILITY

GENERAL DESCRIPTION: You have subjugated your ego and seek genuine feedback and insights from others. You know and appreciate that this will generate better ideas. You have a willingness to listen to and incorporate the insights and ideas of others and not to become defensive when others throw proverbial stones at your thoughts and ideas.

HOW IT MAY LOOK: Humility is important when identifying customer needs or product gaps. Product managers, for example, often have great pride in their offerings and may not have the humility necessary to understand consumers' unmet needs. Humility can lead to greater insight into and discovery of unmet needs, but only if managers let go of their egos and are willing to listen to consumer input.

5. CURIOSITY

GENERAL DESCRIPTION: A person with a beginner's mind is relentlessly curious about customer needs, why things work the way they do, why certain processes or programs exist. Curiosity creates energy for innovative activity. Curiosity helps overcome the organizational inertia that stymies discovery and change.

HOW IT MAY LOOK: You have an interest in nearly all topics, and this compels you to constantly inquire and learn more. You don't just ask questions; you ask probing, timely, challenging, and interesting questions that matter, questions that make people think and want to participate in learning along with you.

6. EXPLORING ATTITUDE

GENERAL DESCRIPTION: You are an explorer of alternative possibilities and love experimenting to learn what works and what doesn't work. You are keenly aware that exploring, like experimenting, is the act of testing different ideas or alternatives to discover either the potential of a solution or the potential of a "successful failure."

HOW IT MAY LOOK: A person with a beginner's mind constantly seeks to explore the scope, depth, and breadth of challenges and needs, and consistently experiments with potential solutions to learn what works to address a need. Advice to coaching managers: explore more and expect less.

> *"Curiosity is, in great and generous minds,*
> *the first passion and the last."*
> —Samuel Johnson

The beginner's mind is able to focus attention on the now, with a lack of ego, defensiveness, or fear of failure. Most importantly, the beginner's mind is neither deceived by what it knows nor defensive about what it doesn't know. This point alone gives it tremendous practical merit in managing and coaching, for one simple reason: by being flexible and non-dogmatic, the coach and the coached are free to approach any challenge or any problem from any angle.

In a sense, the beginner's mind, unlike an expert's mind, is programmed to see possibilities and help people find solutions to *their* challenges. The beginner's mind is the mind of empathy and compassion. When your coaching approach is empathetic and your actions are compassionate, the results are boundless.

EXPERTISE CAN HELP OR HARM

Many of us, when confronted with a challenge or problem, call on everything that we "know" to solve the problem. We turn to accepted solutions, documented examples, and our own experience to build on previous success. But what we fail to recognize is that what we "know" may not always be comprehensively complete, and calling on what we know may only reinforce the conclusions we already have, excluding other information or perspectives.

As Winston Churchill said in 1946 at the University of Miami: "Expert knowledge, however indispensable, is no substitute for a generous and comprehending outlook upon the human story with all its sadness and with all its unquenchable hope."

Expertise can be a great accelerator for managing and coaching success, but it can also become a significant barrier. Knowledge and expertise often signal status and importance. We respect people who can quickly deliver answers and information about challenges, rather than people who ask questions to learn more about a problem. Actively demonstrating a lack of knowledge or rejecting existing knowledge can reduce a person's status or introduce the risk that others will refuse to take them or their ideas seriously.

It should come as no surprise to discover that Steve Jobs attributed some of his success in innovation to the Zen concept of a beginner's mind. He used beginner's mind to radically rethink portable music and cellular phones. Managers can use beginner's mind to rethink existing parameters and models, and to become better coaches. By rejecting what you think you know for certain and approaching an individual or team challenge without preconceptions, you can discover new ways to help people grow and learn.

USE ETC

A manager who has experienced beginner's mind can also help someone else experience it. In addition to its lack of ego, defensiveness, and fear of failure, a beginner's mind is a willing mind: willing to wonder, willing to experience, willing to see details, and, most importantly for a coaching manager, willing to learn.

The irony is that, as children, we were almost constantly in beginner's mind. Unfortunately, our school and work experiences often produce a closed and cautious mind focused on trying to look good, reduce risk, and survive—not exactly an ideal climate for learning and innovation, but a great way to waste vital energy.

When one is attempting to look good, reduce risk, and survive, there is a tendency to wear masks for others and to hide their personal core values—even from themselves. Work realities can harden us and make us cynical and pessimistic.

How does one rediscover their beginner's mind? How can you help someone begin again? Helping someone begin again—to see things with a beginner's mind—requires *ETC:* Empathy, Trust, and Credibility.

Empathy

A coaching manager exudes a unique kind of *empathy* that goes beyond sharing another person's past or present experiences and emotions. The best managers have sensitivity and see someone's future possibilities. Not only can a great coaching manager vicariously experience the feelings and thoughts of someone else's past or present, they can also visualize and articulate a person's potential. A great coaching manager is driven to help people reach their potential.

HOW TO EMPATHIZE

Empathizing establishes a coaching relationship bond that leads to sustainable improvement. To achieve this, follow these three steps.

1. Step outside yourself and listen carefully to the stated and unstated goals, opportunities, and challenges of your team members. Stand in their shoes. Imagine what it is like to feel and think the way they do. Then summarize and paraphrase your understanding back to that person. Use the following types of words: "Help me understand..." or "Based on what you are telling me, here's how it occurs to me..."

2. Refrain from judging a person and remedying all but the most urgent (i.e., life- or business-threatening) issues immediately. Ask questions that help team members understand issues more fully and, as appropriate, give them the resources, autonomy, and accountability to find and implement lasting solutions, with your continued guidance and coaching.

3. Provide honest feedback and the opportunity for learning and continuous improvement as solutions are sought and implemented. This has the potential to help the people reporting to you accumulate and store up energy instead of using their energy reserves for covering up or worrying about your reaction to inevitable mistakes and missteps.

One of the top sports coaches of all time, John Wooden, exemplified this sensitivity to future possibilities. Integral to Coach Wooden's philosophy of success was helping his players reach their full potential, both on the basketball court and as human beings. In Wooden's world, players were competing against an ideal, an abstract standard of excellence defined by the coach. The actual opponents mattered little. It was the ideal that mattered most.

A coaching manager's empathy and sensitivity do not manifest strictly as sympathy or acceptance. A coaching manager uses words and actions to help people see and seek their full potential at work…and in life. Wooden summed up his definition of success in this way: "Success is peace of mind, attained only through self-satisfaction and knowing you made the effort to do the best of what you are capable."

Trust

A successful manager understands that earning *trust* is the gateway to honest dialogue and safe learning. Since learning something new often comes with the risk of being embarrassed, having a trusted and trusting manager as a safety net can be invaluable for achieving sustainable behavior change.

Ultimately, your success as a manager depends on your ability to earn and deserve trust. What can you consistently do to give the people who report to you the information they need to decide whether to trust you? Ultimately trust must be earned.

One of the most effective ways for managers to earn trust is to be a strong, credible communicator. An early manager and coach that I reported to always took the time to communicate across all levels of the organization. She also took the time to get to know everyone directly and indirectly involved with our business unit, especially those who could potentially influence outcomes and decisions that would impact our team. This extra step made it possible for others in the organization to get to know and trust her, and it made it easier for me to accurately and openly communicate strategies and goals to my team.

Credibility

The "C" in ETC stands for *credibility* and means that with predictable regularity you do what you say: you walk your talk. People who know you recognize the consistency of your words and behavior—but that's not enough to be a credible manager. You can say and do things that are consistent and still be a self-centered jerk of a manager. So, you need to add one more requirement: a set of core personal values that prioritize a love of learning and a passion for helping others.

If you are serious about solidifying your trust and credibility, seek to master these five habits:

Seek to master these...	While avoiding these...
1. Do what you say you will do.	Avoid: » Agreeing to something you are not 100 percent sure you can deliver » An over-packed schedule » Excuses » Saying yes to everything
2. Fall in love with learning.	Avoid: » Protecting yourself from making mistakes » Thinking you know enough about something
3. Care more about others than yourself.	Avoid: » Thinking of yourself first and foremost » Making assumptions about other people
4. Be accountable for your actions.	Avoid: » Being a victim » Blaming others
5. Be humble.	Avoid: » Taking full credit for anything » Setting yourself up as a know-it-all

DISCIPLINE 1 SUMMARY

If you are serious about improving your managing and coaching skills and about climbing the first discipline of the Coaching Ladder, you must approach problems and opportunities with a *beginner's mind*. Practice ETC to help someone else develop this beginner's mind: 1) resurrect your *empathetic self;* 2) earn *trust;* and 3) strengthen your *credibility.* All the great managers have an acute awareness of ETC—not solely for altruistic reasons, but for the sake of good old ROI. The coaching and managing you provide to your team members will pay off. Big time.

ENERGIZERS

Here are some reinforcing and energizing ideas to consider when practicing Discipline 1: Begin Again.

If you want someone to have the will to learn...help them take on a beginner's mind.

✔ *Have a conversation about trust.*

The person you manage has to trust you. Reassure them that you have their back—you will keep all coaching conversations private and confidential. Make certain they know it's okay to make mistakes, as long as they are willing to talk about what they have learned.

✅ *Find out if they really want to change.*

The greatest manager in the world cannot help people who don't want to help themselves. Ask questions: Are you committed to doing something different to get better results? Why? How will you demonstrate this commitment?

✅ *"If your mother says she loves you, check it out."*

This management adage exists for good reason. The principle behind it—effective management requires a dose of skepticism—can keep you from relying solely on what the person being managed tells you in early meetings. Ask if you can observe them in a variety of situations over time and/or if they can commit to regular coaching conversations.

> *"It's what you learn after you know it all that counts."*
> —Attributed to Harry S. Truman

> *"You learn something every day if you pay attention."*
> —Ray LeBlond

> *"Some people will never learn anything …*
> *because they understand everything too soon."*
> —Alexander Pope

DISCIPLINE 2:
KNOW YOURSELF

"Anyone can plot a course with a map or compass; but without a sense of who you are, you will never know if you're already home."
—Shannon L. Alder

"He who knows others is learned; he who knows himself is wise."
—Lao Tzu, Tao Te Ching

"The thing that is really hard, and really amazing, is giving up on being perfect and beginning the work of becoming yourself."
—Anna Quindlen

I first met Scott Riley on a hot and muggy Monday at a distribution center in Charlotte, North Carolina. He was the U.S. head of distribution for a global supplier in the food and restaurant industry. It was the first day we met—I was the coach and Scott was the client. But as with most of my coaching assignments, I would learn just as much from Scott as he did from me.

During our introductory meeting, I remember asking Scott about who he was: What would you like to accomplish? What is most important to you, and why? What do you think your core personal values are? Generally, upon an initial coaching encounter, no matter how smooth or complete the answer, I ask the people I coach to give this last question further thought and reflection for discussion at our next meeting. I might even provide a "values activity" to help someone discover their three core values. But with Scott, I got my answer right away. He dug into his right front pocket and handed me a small metal object.

This round, well-worn metal pin—about the size of a dime—did not belong to Scott, although, as he explained, it was given to him. On the pin were nothing else but three gold-colored capital letters: PLC. Scott's grandfather had given the pin to his father, who had in turn given it to Scott.

Scott assumed that the speech he heard from his father was the same one his grandfather had given to his dad: "Congratulations, son. You are now a member of the Perpetual Learners Club. Not everyone is a member of this club, but anyone can be a member. As a member, you have but one responsibility: never stop learning."

With these brief words and the PLC pin, Scott explained that the most important personal value for him was an insatiable and humble curiosity about the people and things that came into his life. Whenever he looked at the pin—his silent companion—it became his compass. It was a symbolic reminder to avoid ideological ruts, feelings of superiority, or a false sense that something had been mastered.

Since he received the pin, Scott explained, his foot was always on the learning pedal, always endeavoring to glean more about the nature and background of people and things. Needless to say, I did not assign Scott any "learn your own personal values" activities. One more thing: During the time I was coaching Scott, his wife gave birth to their first child—a child who I'm certain was destined to receive the PLC pin someday.

BE A PERPETUAL LEARNER

Most of us haven't achieved what Scott discovered and what was memorialized by the PLC pin. Most of us don't live life as a perpetual learner. The simple skills and abilities to live life in this way at work are absent for too many managers.

Dr. W. Edwards Deming put it this way when he wrote the following to Peter Senge:

> *Our prevailing system of management has destroyed our people. People are born with intrinsic motivation, self-respect, dignity, curiosity to learn, joy in learning. The forces of destruction begin with toddlers—a prize for the best Halloween costume, grades in school, gold stars—and on up through the university. On the job, people, teams, and divisions are ranked, reward for the top, punishment for the bottom…Quotas, incentive pay, business plans, put together separately, division by division, cause further loss, unknown and unknowable.* (From the article, "The Management Thinker We Should Never Have Forgotten," *Harvard Business Review*)

The "systematizing of management" that Deming refers to results in culturally-embedded beliefs and practices profoundly inconsistent with human beings' innate desire to learn. How strong is this desire to learn? "The drive to learn," said anthropologist Edward T. Hall, "is more basic than the drive to reproduce." But our primary institutions—work and school—are designed to control and avoid mistakes, and minimize out-of-the-box creativity and impactful innovation.

LEARNING AND CONTROL

The profound mismatch between our innate drive to learn and our organization's drive to control thwarts curiosity, invention, experimentation, and a sense of connection. It is one of your primary roles to help people get back in touch with the profound sense of wonder and the thrill of learning. *You cannot have a sense of wonder if you are prepared for everything, if you are constantly on patrol for control.* The entryway to learning begins with questions. And a legendary coaching manager asks lots of interesting questions.

ESSENTIAL QUESTIONS

There are also some questions every manager should ask themselves. For example, what are *my* core personal values? It's an important question, and one coaching managers ask themselves, as well as others. How am I *really* doing? There are many ways to answer this seemingly trite question. As always, context is king. Would your answer to a boss who asks you this at work be different than to a friend who poses the question at a party? What if you had a trusted manager who asked you?

Here are other questions: What sustains me? What provides a foundation when challenges and obstacles arise? And where does this sustainability come from?

SAFE, SUSTAINABLE PLACE

Each of us, wherever we are in our lives, has something that sustains us. You won't find it by looking over your shoulder, although it is often right beside you, waiting to be called upon. You will find it in a "safe, sustainable place" reserved only for you.

One of my first legendary managers—someone I reported to for four years—discovered his special, sustainable place was in the quiet moments at home in his music room, where he ultimately decided to come out to the world as a gay man. "I discovered the person I am and want to be comes to life when I have the courage to be honest—honest with myself, honest with others, honest in my business practices."

I learned an important lesson from this manager: to cherish and keep close a safe, sustainable place, where you can always go to find and rediscover who you are and what you value. I have often found that place when playing a competitive sport.

THE RIGHT KINDS OF QUESTIONS

A good manager asks questions. A coach asks questions to make you think. For example:

» When you've been away from work for a while, what do you miss the most?

» What is the worst thing about yourself that you like?

» What is the greatest lesson you have ever learned?

» Do you have the opportunity to do what you do best each and every day?

» What is holding you back from achieving your goals?

» When have you been emotionally committed to something?

» Why were you emotionally committed?

» What has had the most profound impact on your life, and what has it changed in you?

» Why do you think this had such a profound impact on you?

» Who do you admire most and why?

» How has failure shaped your approach to life?

When I was younger, basketball and skiing calmed me down, and I noticed after a competitive game on the court or a day on a mountain, I was able to concentrate better on what was most important in my life. The Danish philosopher Søren Kierkegaard wrote in an 1847 letter, "Health and salvation can only be found in motion." I can't be sure about the salvation part, but I know without regular and vigorous physical activity, I'd be more restless and irritable at home and work—and more inclined to brood about things.

A safe, sustainable place can be anywhere, and it will be different for everyone. Laetitia Williams, one of the first employees I ever managed and coached, found the place where she felt she came to life with an inner calm representing her better self. This place came in her relationship with her severely handicapped daughter, a daughter she was raising as a single mom with help from round-the-clock caregivers.

"It's hard to describe the depth of the inner calm welling up inside when I am caring for my daughter. The deep love for and bond with my daughter— when I'm reading to her, bathing her, watching over her as she goes to sleep— give me insight into what it means to have perspective. It's hard to describe how free I feel at work because of my ability to look at any situation and determine what is most important."

The deep perspective found in that safe, sustainable place gave Laetitia the insights that she could not always control what happened, but she could always control her attitude toward it.

How would you fill in this blank: "The person I truly am or truly want to be comes to life when I'm _____." Does this come down to one word or several? The word or words you choose help identify what sustains you, provides meaning for you, and helps you better understand who you are and what you stand for.

One of the most common obstacles to successful performance at work is *not* knowing yourself: your personality, strengths, weaknesses, and blind spots. Coaching managers help people learn about themselves and, most importantly, how to manage themselves. We all have a gap between who we are and who we think we are, between who we might be and who we want to be. Managers have to be sensitive to this. A big part of this sensitivity is learning about 1) someone's past and current self-image; 2) their dreams for the future; and 3) how others see them. The poet John Masefield describes the importance of recognizing these three images of the "self":

> And there were three men
> Went down the road as down the road went he.
> The man they saw,
> The man he was,
> The man he wanted to be.

CULTIVATING SELF-UNDERSTANDING

The main idea here is simple: the coaching manager wants people to focus on their strengths and cultivate a deep understanding of who they are. As a manager who coaches, you want to help people understand where they can make the greatest contribution to their organization, as well as to their family, friends, and community.

The people you manage need to learn how to go deeper into themselves than mere insights into strengths and weaknesses. They also need to understand how they learn, how they fit in and work with others, what their core personal values are, and where they can make the greatest contribution. Only then will they have the potential to achieve true and sustainable excellence.

Many people don't really know who they are or what causes them to do what they do. Do you know how your interpersonal needs influence your communication style and behavior? Do you know what your talents are? Have you been able to leverage or tap into your natural skills in your current role? Have you discovered the relatively stable set of characteristics and tendencies making up your unique personality?

Coaching managers have a seemingly insatiable desire to help people learn about themselves. Fortunately, it's also true these managers are self-aware and have a strong desire to learn as much as they can about themselves.

Successful managers:

» Know what they are good at.
» Are able to honestly list their own unique abilities and weaknesses.
» Recognize they are not masters of everything.
» Get feedback from others on a regular basis.
» Hire and retain talent that supplements and complements their strengths and weaknesses.

ASSESSMENT INSTRUMENTS

There are many assessment tools to help managers and leaders better understand their interpersonal needs and how those needs influence their communication style and behavior—and, in the process, improve their personal relationships and professional performance.

Most of these tools sharpen an understanding of one's own perceptions and judgments; they also clarify how *others* perceive and judge. If people differ systematically in what they perceive and how they reach conclusions, then it is only reasonable they will differ correspondingly in their interests, reactions, values, motivations, and skills.

Managing is both a science and an art, the focus of which is ultimately human nature, which is in great part consistent and measurable. When something works again and again, it can become a rule; not necessarily a scientific law, but a rule of thumb. But this doesn't mean something different won't be as or more effective.

There is a friendly and spirited debate today within several of the management communities I belong to about when and how to use assessment instruments. Some believe only certified assessors can and should provide feedback, while others believe there are validated instruments allowing any manager to self-assess, without the need for a certified expert.

What I have picked up during these lively debates is a streak of conservatism within many veteran managers—especially those who want only certified assessors to provide validated feedback. I don't mean conservative in the ideological sense of the word. The veteran practitioners tend to stick with what they have seen work.

I'm somewhat in the middle in this debate. Some tests or assessments clearly do require an expert to properly interpret and understand the results at a deep level, and then to help someone take action on this understanding. Assessments, like any other tool, can either hurt or heal. Psychologists I know who have studied psychometrics refer to assessments as being an "imperfect mirror" of how someone sees themselves.

The Fundamental Interpersonal Relations Orientation™ (FIRO-B®) and the array of Hogan assessment systems would be examples of tools requiring the expertise of someone certified in these instruments.

On the other hand, using a certified resource for feedback and analysis is not the only way to discover your strengths and areas where improvement is needed. If an "expert" is not available to assist with this analysis, does that mean your strengths and opportunities should remain undiscovered forever? Of course not.

While an expert can add value to the feedback and analysis process an assessment facilitates, the following assessment tools can be used by anyone willing to take the time to understand their origins, purposes, and proper interpretations: Myers-Briggs Type Indicator® (MBTI®), Clifton StrengthsFinder®, and The PACE® Palette. While these are valid and useful tools, they often miss one of the more critical aspects of being an effective manager and coach: critical-thinking and problem-solving capacity.

In your ascent up this second rung of the Coaching Ladder—Know Yourself (p. 4)—you are making a practical journey to learning a few simple ideas, techniques, and tools to help people learn about themselves—and you don't need to be a certified expert to do this.

Of course, before you can help someone else, you must first practice what you are about to preach. The Self-Assessment Roadmap described over the next several pages will take you on such a critical journey of self-discovery.

By practicing this discipline, you will have the facts, perceptions, and clues to help you set your destination on the third discipline of the Coaching Ladder. This will in turn enable you to set goals with your team members that are aligned with your organization's strategic intent.

THE SELF-ASSESSMENT ROADMAP

1. Complete the Intake Questionnaire.
2. Complete at least two assessment instruments.
3. Summarize what you have learned:
   a. What are my strengths?
   b. How do I learn?
   c. What are my personal core values?
   d. What are my "blind spots"?

Complete the Intake Questionnaire

What it is: The Intake Questionnaire is a tool for sharing life-story details and scratching the surface of perceived strengths, gaps, and goals. I ask every person I coach to fill out the questionnaire prior to our first coaching session. While it might seem awkward for you to employ this format and use the same approach I do with my clients, the key is to think about and develop a strategy for getting to know someone. What is most important to them—at work and outside of work? Where do they want to be in the future? It's fine to adjust the questions shown on the sample intake form and ask them at the right moment, after you have established the level of trust described earlier.

Why it's important: The questionnaire encourages honest and healthy self-reflection from the person answering the questions and from the coaching manager. The answers provide a great start in getting to know the person you're managing: their aspirations, self-perceived strengths, and areas to improve, as well

[?]

INTAKE QUESTIONNAIRE

» Who are the most important people in your life?

» What are your core personal values?

» Using bullet points, write your life story.

» List at least five of your personal strengths and assets.

» List at least three things you are willing to improve or change.

» List three things holding you back (e.g., bad habits, limiting beliefs, recurring problems, personal circumstances).

» Describe how you want your life to be in three years.

» Project: Create a photograph, or series of photos, showing ten favorite things in your life.

as what they would like to accomplish through the coaching process and other equally important concerns.

How you can use this tool: Before you pose these questions to someone else, use the tool to 1) get to know yourself better and focus your own thinking; 2) help you clarify your own goals; and 3) become comfortable with the questions so you can use the questionnaire with other people you manage.

Look to your strengths. From the Gallup research and the retail business-case example on the following page, it's not difficult to figure out my bias when it comes to assessments: look first to your strengths! And the only way to truly discover your strengths is through independent, validated analysis.

LOOK TO YOUR STRENGTHS FIRST

Several years ago, a leading retailer invited my company to administer and implement their first employee-engagement survey. The company owned and operated more than 1,500 stores across the U.S. The survey data showed a strong correlation between operational and financial metrics (e.g., same-store sales, customer loyalty index, volume, gross margin) and high engagement among team members and shift managers. Stores with high engagement scores consistently achieved annual targets and far outpaced stores with low team- and manager-engagement scores.

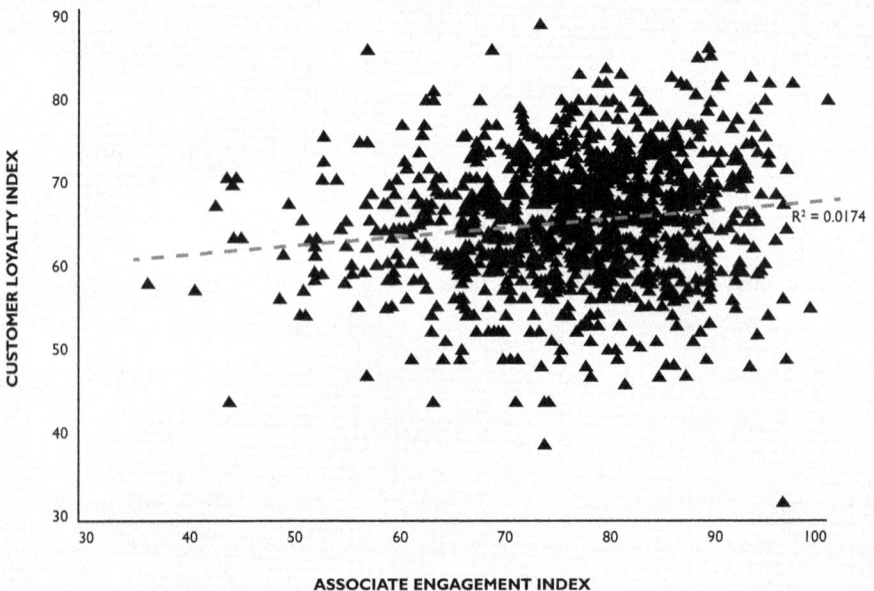

$R^2 = 0.0174$

CUSTOMER LOYALTY INDEX

ASSOCIATE ENGAGEMENT INDEX

The CEO decided to make two simultaneous investments: 1) in the top ten high-engagement/high-results stores and 2) in the bottom ten low-engagement/low-results stores. The same amount of "improvement money" was devoted to each store for one year, and, in most cases, very similar solutions were provided: for example, an internal operations SWAT team sent from the home office to provide consulting and advice to each store for two weeks; quarterly shift-manager training and development; and design and implementation of employee-orientation and -retention strategies.

A second engagement survey was implemented eighteen months after the first one, and the results were revealing: every store in the top and bottom tiers of the first survey increased their engagement scores and improved operational and financial metrics. But there was an important difference between the original top ten stores and bottom ten stores: The top ten increased engagement scores by an average of 24 percent. The bottom ten increased engagement scores by a mere 5 percent. The percentage difference was similar for operational and financial metrics. The headline: a focus on strengths achieves far greater benefits than a focus on weaknesses.

Complete at Least Two Assessment Instruments

Most managers think they know what they are good at. They rose through the ranks through their ability to achieve results, get credit for those results, and maintain relationships with people who have organizational power and prestige. Ask managers what they are good at, and they will be happy to tell you. They are usually wrong.

Strengths and opportunities to improve. Do you know what you are good at—what your strengths are? Would you bet the proverbial house on it? Managers think they know their strengths, but, more often than not, what they actually know is what they are *not* good at—their weaknesses. After multiple feedback and evaluation sessions with their bosses, most managers are well aware of these "opportunities to improve." And they are sick and tired of living in a business world relentlessly focused on fixing perceived weaknesses.

As Peter F. Drucker once wrote, "One cannot build performance on weakness, let alone on something one cannot do at all." As a manager, you must become aware of your strengths, and how to grow and leverage those strengths, in order to know where you can best add value—to your business, to your team, and for yourself. Research from Gallup indicates people have several times greater potential for growth when they focus energy on developing their strengths instead of on fixing weaknesses. This same message also holds true for the different business units, locations, and teams within an organization.

Summarize What You Have Learned

What are your strengths? The assessments were designed to help you identify and validate some of the strengths or talents you possess. The best tactic for improvement is to focus on just one or two, rather than all, of your strengths. What are the three most important words in real estate? Location. Location. Location. The three most important words for self-improvement, or when helping someone else improve, are: Focus. Focus. Focus. Focus will make your strongest traits even stronger.

How do *you* learn? In her book *How Your Child Is Smart*, Dr. Dawna Markova identifies personal thinking patterns determining the most comfortable and effective way for each of us to learn something new. These patterns are anchored by three primary channels of thought and experience: visual, auditory, and kinesthetic. How we learn—whether someone primarily uses one or another of these three channels—is another vital piece of information to learn about yourself and others. Of all the important pieces of the puzzle of self-knowledge, understanding how you learn is the easiest to acquire. Using the characteristics on the list on the next page,

Visual Learner Characteristics

- ❑ Remember what they see, rather than what they hear.
- ❑ Remember diagrams and pictures.
- ❑ Prefer to read and write, rather than listen.
- ❑ Have trouble remembering verbal instructions.
- ❑ Need an overall view and purpose before beginning a project.
- ❑ Prefer visual art to music.

Auditory Learner Characteristics

- ❑ Remember by listening, especially to music.
- ❑ Distracted by noise.
- ❑ Write lightly and sometimes illegibly.
- ❑ Remember names, but forget faces.
- ❑ Find games and pictures annoying and distracting.

Kinesthetic Learner Characteristics

- ❑ Speak with their hands and gestures.
- ❑ Remember what was done but have difficulty recalling what was said or seen.
- ❑ Will try new things.
- ❑ Rely on what they can directly experience, do, or perform.
- ❑ Are naturally outgoing and expressive.
- ❑ Need to be active and in motion.

check off which characteristics are more "true" for you or someone you manage. Most people will have some check marks under each of the three characteristics, but typically one characteristic will predominate.

What are _your_ personal core values? Author Stan Slap has demonstrated the link between personal values, leadership, and emotional commitment in his articles and books. If you understand this connection, you will become a better manager and coach. Identifying and living _your_ core personal values are the

INSIGHTS ON STRENGTHS AND WEAKNESSES

Thinking about strengths first and weaknesses second is not as easy as it may sound. I sometimes think humans are wired to focus first on the negative, to overemphasize mistakes and perceived "weaknesses." The ability to prioritize the negative over the positive is probably evolutionary. From our earliest beginnings, being aware of and avoiding danger has been a critical survival skill.

Psychologists Paul Rozin and Edward Royzman have shown in their research on "negativity bias" a negative perspective is more contagious than a positive perspective. Other researchers have shown our attitudes are more heavily influenced by bad news than good. It's no wonder there are more emotional words that are negative (62 percent) than positive (32 percent) in the English dictionary.

Research has demonstrated there are two different systems in our brains for negative and positive stimuli. The amygdala, part of the emotional limbic system, uses approximately two-thirds of its neurons to detect negative experiences. Once the brain comes upon bad news, it is stored into long-term memory nearly instantaneously. Positive experiences, on the other hand, have to be held in our awareness for more than twelve seconds to transfer completely from short-term to long-term memory. Dr. Rick Hanson describes it in this way: "In effect, the brain is like Velcro for negative experiences but Teflon for positive ones. That shades 'implicit memory'—your underlying expectations, beliefs, action strategies, and mood—in an increasingly negative direction."

There is a tool I have used for more than twenty years with individuals and teams that illustrates this aspect of being human: The Contingency Diagram.

The tool invites people to focus on negative outcomes first. I once used this tool with a team of engineers focused on launching unmanned rockets into space. "What if our goal was to ensure this unmanned spacecraft launches and *never* successfully delivers the communication satellite and hosted payload module?" I asked. "What actions would have to occur for this new goal to happen?" Since focusing on the negative often comes more easily to both individuals and teams, this approach legitimizes negativity and says it's okay get the negatives out first...and have some fun doing so. The list of "negative stuff" is usually long, and the important step of turning these ideas around into something positive and preventative—the "contingencies"—typically yields a much higher-quality list of actions than if you start out asking: "What are all the things we have to get right to make this a successful launch?"

foundational steps to fulfillment at work and unleashing emotional commitment within yourself and others. To quote Slap:

> "The irreducible essence of leadership is that leaders are people who live their deepest personal values without compromise, and they use those values to make life better for others—this is why people become leaders and why people follow leaders." (*Bury My Heart at Conference Room B*)

What are *your* "blind spots"? When my son turned one, I made two observations: 1) He was perfectly capable of, and actually quite proficient at, walking full speed into a wall without slowing down to mitigate the impending collision. This went on for many days, and I began to wonder about him until I saw many of his playmates the same age doing the same thing (all males, I might add; I never saw a one-year-old girl do this). 2) He would attempt to pick up the holes and black shadows on cement sidewalks and driveways. He would carefully and thoughtfully reach down and squeeze the dark spot with his thumb and forefinger. He would repeat this a few times, and then look at me as if to say: "What the hell?" Eventually, he outgrew these little blind spots and found other ways to worry his parents, or to crack them up.

When it comes to the business environment, blind spots are unproductive or destructive behaviors invisible to the people doing them but glaringly obvious to the team members around them. Examples of blind spots I see in my coaching practice include taking too long to get to the point, assuming "more" is better than "less" in presentations and speeches, an inability to let go and hold others accountable, not understanding the difference between running and growing a business, and lack of attention to an industry's big picture and strategic landscape.

It is often your role to look for and help others address their blind spots. You help someone become more self-aware, which can lead to the willingness to address the blind spot. Here are two common blind spots and advice on ways to tackle and change "blind spot" behavior.

1. Inability to ask for help. It is not uncommon for someone to feel they are expected to do it all, and even to believe they *can* do it all. Some of your team members may have a tendency to isolate themselves and not involve or enlist the support of peers, even when really needed. Asking for help can be perceived as a sign of weakness or ignorance. Another common barrier is nervousness about incurring political obligations at work: "What will I owe this person now?" For American workers in particular, cultural values can get in the way. Self-reliance is an admirable trait, but it can also be self-limiting.

MAKING IT EASY FOR PEOPLE TO CONTRIBUTE IDEAS

One of my coaching clients, the chief operating officer for a global media and entertainment company, created a simple structured tool to help people think about what they want and easily ask for help to solve problems and pursue opportunities, large or small. He realized once people could clearly articulate what they wanted and needed at work, it was easier for them to ask. And he had an idea for a tool that could help them do this.

The tool was a simplified version of a cost-benefit analysis, and the best part of it was anyone in the organization could access the one-page template and use it at any time. He called it "CBI" (Cost-Benefit and Is It Worth It?). It soon became a legendary cultural icon in the company and helped streamline early "go/no go" decisions for a variety of film and music projects, publishing, and pie-in-the-sky requests.

Coaching advice: First, recognize an inability to ask for help is very different from not wanting help. There is often very little you can do as a manager or coach for someone who does not want to be helped.

Second, consider if you have fostered an environment in your team or department that encourages asking for help. Many creative design firms have strong norms that make asking for and giving help a virtue. In this *culture of helping,* designers are coached from the start to recognize they will need help and to ask for it. Watching others give and get help reinforces norms and creates a feeling of psychological safety.

Third, ask yourself this question: What am I doing to help team members clearly articulate what they want? This all-too-obvious step is often overlooked. Not everyone has a clear view of the help they need. The more clarity they have about what they want, the better. Help people who report to you take the time to learn, figure out, and discover exactly what they want and need, and then make it safe for them to ask.

2. The need to be right. Some people feel always being "right" translates to being successful. They will expend their competitive energy, time, and resources just to prove they are right about something…perhaps everything. Many organizations, and too many of our education systems, are rooted in constructs of right and wrong. We are rewarded for "correct" answers and penalized for being "incorrect." Being right affirms and inflates our sense of self-worth. We have learned to avoid, as best we can, the embarrassment of being wrong. Getting the right answer becomes the primary purpose of our education systems and all too often of our organizations as well. But this is inconsistent with learning.

Coaching advice: If you know someone who has this tendency, ask them to step back and consider the consequences of not being right. Find the right time to ask questions like: Are you shutting out other options or possible courses of action? What additional information might you be missing by not considering other options? What opportunities are you cutting off for yourself and your team? If you were wrong, does it mean you've failed or you've learned something?

DISCIPLINE 2 SUMMARY

Growth starts by understanding your strengths and determining what you need to unlearn. People perform from strengths. The managers who also coach want people to focus on their strengths and cultivate a deep understanding of who they are, including what they need to do differently. The people you manage need to learn how to look deeper into themselves rather than focus on insights solely about their strengths and weaknesses. They also need to understand how they learn, how they fit in and work with others, what their core personal values are, and where they can make the greatest contribution. Only then will they have the potential to achieve true, sustainable excellence. Learning new things is the easy part. Letting go of what used to work in years past but is no longer relevant to today's reality is much harder.

ENERGIZERS

Here are some reinforcing and energizing ideas to consider when practicing Discipline 2: Know Yourself.

If you want someone to understand their strengths and opportunities...

✅ **Help people learn about themselves.**
The best coaching managers create a foundation of trust and authenticity from which they form lasting relationships with those they coach. Provide subjective

feedback—from the heart—to the person you are coaching while recommending more objective methods of identifying strengths and improvement opportunities.

✅ Help people discover their values and strengths.

Help the people you manage and coach discover their core personal values: ask them to read Stan Slap's book *Bury My Heart at Conference Room B* and complete the values exercise in Part 3. Help them discover their own personal strengths: share Tom Rath's *StrengthsFinder 2.0,* and help them complete and interpret the online inventory.

✅ Summarize strengths and opportunities to improve.

Co-create a "T-chart" showing strengths on the left and areas for improvement on the right. Co-create a "From/To" chart showing desired movement from current behavior to future behavior. Ask these questions: What do you value most about yourself? What inspires you? What lessons do you find yourself learning over and over again? What skills do others say you need to develop?

> *"People often say that this or that person has not yet found himself. But the self is not something one finds, it is something one creates."*
> —Thomas Szasz

> *"There is only one corner of the universe you can be certain of improving, and that's your own self."*
> —Aldous Huxley

DISCIPLINE 3:
ALIGN DESTINATION

"You've got to think about big things while you're doing small things, so that all the small things go in the right direction."
—Alvin Toffler

"If you don't know where you are going, you'll end up someplace else."
—Yogi Berra

"It is not enough to do your best; you must first know what to do, and then do your best."
—W. Edwards Deming

As a frequent facilitator of offsite management, planning, and learning events, I have been in front of thousands of managers over the years. Every time the topic of motivation is raised, the following questions come up: "How can I motivate my team to achieve more?" "How can I motivate an underperformer?" "What can I do to motivate my direct reports to 'row' in the same direction?"

My first response to these questions tends to put managers back on their heels: "You can't motivate anyone, any team, or any group, so take that heavy stone off your back right now."

Obviously, my message is a little too black and white. If we define motivation as the desire or willingness to act or behave in a particular way, there are many examples of managers who are able to motivate individuals and teams. When this is done with the proverbial "carrot and stick," that's what's known as *extrinsic* motivation.

The best motivation, however, comes from the inside: *intrinsic* motivation. The basic premise is individuals are accountable for motivating themselves, and others can't motivate you intrinsically any more than you can motivate them. However, a manager can help create an environment in which people can find motivation within. This may sound like a subtle difference, but the implications are profound.

Intrinsic Motivation: A person is intrinsically motivated if the desire for change comes from within. The person may want to learn something because he or she is interested. Another person may want to accomplish a goal or task because it is something he or she feels competent at or enjoys doing.

Extrinsic Motivation: On the other hand, extrinsic motivation comes from outside. People are bribed to do something or earn a prize or reward if they meet a goal. Paychecks are extrinsic motivators, as are fear of punishment and coercion.

MOTIVATION AND GOAL SETTING

When I have conversations with managers about motivation, my assumption is they should be focused on creating the conditions for intrinsic motivation to occur: helping generate that spark of motivation that comes from within. This is the motivation that moves mountains and creates the conditions for sustained emotional commitment and the possibility of measurable change.

If you can help an individual or your team *strike another match*—start something new, establish a new goal, or change a long-standing habit getting in the way of innovative thinking or results—you will be grappling with the key question on this third rung of the Coaching Ladder: "Change *from* what *to* what?"

GOAL SETTING PROS AND CONS

In the late 1960s, Edwin A. Locke and Gary P. Latham's pioneering research on goal setting and motivation produced several findings all coaches should be aware of:

» Setting specific, difficult goals leads to higher performance than merely urging people to do their best.

» Higher goals generate greater effort than lower goals, and the highest or most difficult goals produce the greatest levels of effort and performance.

» Making a public commitment to a goal enhances personal commitment.

Other researchers, however, caution against too much goal setting. Professor Lisa Ordoñez and her colleagues at the University of Arizona warn overprescribing goal setting as a motivational and performance-enhancing tool can produce negative side effects, including an overly narrow focus that neglects considerations not directly related to goals and distorts risk preferences. Rather than dispensing goal setting as a benign, over-the-counter treatment for "lack of motivation," managers should conceptualize goal setting as a prescription-strength medication that requires careful dosing, consideration of harmful side effects, and close supervision. Ordoñez's research serves as a warning label that should accompany the practice of goal setting.

The manager who coaches helps individuals and teams find and articulate the personal "what" that is right for them *and* is also aligned with the strategy and goals of the organization. The right "what" has the potential to unleash the self-motivation and energy of individuals and teams to become goal drivers, goal seekers, goal obsessives, or—well, fill in your favorite goal cliché.

How much of the current popularity of coaching can be attributed to the interrelationship, and delicate dance, between strengthening an inter-personal relationship and getting results? Are you most interested in coaching because you will be measurably helping someone fulfill their potential or because coaching gives you the best opportunity to finally crack the code on a major challenge or opportunity at your organization? When coaching is done right—when you prepare and naturally integrate it into your role as manager—all either-or questions about this false choice are rendered irrelevant.

The coaching approach prescribed in this book offers the best way to help someone achieve their potential and dreams and get results that add value to your organization. In the first two chapters, the focus was on you. In this chapter you start the tactical step of aligning the hopes *and* dreams of the people and teams you manage to the requirements and strategies of the business.

Imagine what can be accomplished when everyone you coach is working on tasks and projects that, when completed, will help them achieve what they want and what your organization wants. That is the driving practical force of strategic coaching alignment, and your skills and abilities to leverage this force are vital for your ultimate success as a manager. This is not a theory. When the people on your team believe there is a solid through-line between getting what they want most and helping the organization reach and surpass what it wants, they will be on the path toward the kind of emotional commitment that moves mountains for their team, their organization, and you, their manager-coach.

Alignment begins when the people on your team first identify and understand what is most important to them. From the coaching perspective, one of the best ways to help an individual or a team visualize, articulate, and document what they want is to follow these three steps:

1. Start with "what if?"
2. Write a draft of the desired destination, without restriction and inhibition.
3. Align the destination with "smarter" criteria.

Start with "What If?"

Sometimes a good starting point for finding the "what" is to imagine "what if...?"

» What if our team reached its full potential? What would that look like? What would be accomplished?

» What if I could look back on the coming year and was able to say it was my greatest year ever in business? What would have happened?

» What if the sky really was the limit for this new idea of ours? What would the result be?

By asking others to visualize achieving a goal that will produce desired results, you are behaving like a manager *and* a coach: you are helping them focus on what *they* want, first and foremost.

Starting with the "what if" question can help the individual or team you are managing produce a glimpse into a desired future: a future imagined entirely by them, without any unnecessary, inessential, or external voices to cloud or blur the vision.

Rather than jolt the *goal dreamer* back to reality with boundaries and rules, the next step encourages further creativity and free expression, without the restrictions and inhibitions sinking too many *goal searchers*. (The goal clichés just keep on coming!)

Write a Draft of the Desired Destination, without Restriction and Inhibition

After the "what if"ing, and the imagining or reimagining of a desired future, it's time to start writing a goal statement. This may be the most important step in this simple, though not simplistic, goal-setting process. Why? Because you must find an effective and efficient method of stressing the importance of kicking out all restrictions or "goal jams" (with apologies to the rock band MC5). During this second-stage goal writing, you don't want concerns about goal criteria and judgments to get in the way of allowing the rawest and most creative thoughts to surface. For example…

Writing without restriction case study. I recently coached Jane Lyons, an EVP at a leading software company, who used 360-degree-feedback data to learn how others perceive her at work. One of the things she discovered was her peers and direct reports had the perception she was "defensive": when challenged, her *modus operandi* was to resist, defend her actions, and stick to her opinions, no matter what.

When I met with Jane to review the 360 results, "being too defensive" was one of the common themes noted by her direct reports and something she specifically wanted to improve. "I really don't think I'm overly defensive, and I certainly don't want people to think I'm not open to other opinions and ways of doing things," I remember her telling me.

We decided this was worth working on and the next logical step would be to write an improvement or developmental goal focused on this issue. She was familiar with writing "smart" goals, but I told her it was way too early to start applying any criteria of that kind to creating the goal.

As simple and effective as this method can be—and we'll go into it in detail later—it won't help forge an early and strong emotional connection to a goal. Without such a connection, a person is less likely to experience intrinsic motivation.

I explained to Jane it was easy to see why "smart" goals became popular: they are clear and concise, and we now have research showing smart goals can

HISTORY OF SMART

It is generally accepted the SMART acronym first appeared in print in November 1981. George T. Doran, a consultant and former director of corporate planning for the Washington Water Power Company in Spokane, published a paper titled, "There's a S.M.A.R.T. Way to Write Management's Goals and Objectives."

In his paper, Doran provides clarification on how to apply the SMART acronym: "How do you write meaningful objectives?... when it comes to writing effective objectives, corporate officers, managers, and supervisors just have to think of the acronym SMART."

SMART doesn't have a single, definitive meaning. In fact, the words whose initials comprise the acronym have changed over time, and they continue to vary somewhat depending on who is using the term.

Doran's original definition tied in the following five criteria:

» **Specific:** Target a specific area for improvement.

» **Measurable:** Quantify, or at least suggest, an indicator of progress.

» **Assignable:** Specify who will do it.

» **Realistic:** State what results can realistically be achieved given available resources.

» **Time-related:** Specify when the result can be achieved.

NEVER COACH ON AN EMPTY STOMACH

save time and simplify the process of setting measurable objectives. On the other hand, as just mentioned, they don't necessarily guarantee the creation of an emotional bond between goal writers and their goals.

A better approach to the beginning of the goal-setting process is to let go of any restrictions, inhibitions, and criteria that can hinder the free-flowing process of creating a first-draft goal. I asked Jane to go through the following exercise:

> » Think about the perception others have that your behavior tells them you are "defensive":
>   » First, what's wrong with that? Is anything wrong with that?
>   » Why would you want to change that?
>   » What behaviors might cause people to perceive someone or anyone as defensive?
> » Next, think about the opposite of "defensive": how would you describe someone who demonstrates behaviors opposite of "defensive behaviors"?
> » Third, visualize a movie or a series of still pictures in which you are clearly performing these nondefensive behaviors in your interactions with peers and direct reports. What does this look like? What does it feel like—both for them and for you?
> » Lastly, write what you want to improve based on this feedback about becoming or being defensive. Don't worry about grammar. Don't worry about perfection. Don't worry about length. Most of all, don't worry about either you or your goal fitting any specific criteria for success.

With the above steps in mind, Jane wrote a first-draft goal, produced solely for the two of us to review:

Draft 1: Have an open mind and don't be dismissive. Welcome criticism and challenges. Actively ask people to disagree or find problems with what I say and present. Become known for openness and patience.

We talked about this first draft, played around with it, and came up with a second draft that started to get her very interested in achieving the goal:

Draft 2: I will have an open mind that values all opinions and feedback from everyone I work with. I will solicit and welcome feedback, criticism, new ideas, and challenges as opportunities for me to learn. I will be known for openness, patience, and listening.

Notice the differences and similarities. Also notice this is not all science. This goal is not specific enough yet. It would be tough to measure. But it's at a stage where Jane felt good about moving in the direction implied in the draft goal statement.

At the root of this process is the coaching manager, who wants the individual or team first and foremost to own the goal and feel an emotional connection with it. Every individual's general goal of "not being defensive" should and will ultimately be unique.

Align the Destination with "Smarter" Criteria

Around the time of the second or third draft of the goal statement, I introduced—or in this case reintroduced—"smart" criteria but with the slight twist I have added to the tool over the years. The "A" became *Aligned,* and two letters were added to make the goal "smart<u>er</u>." The additional two criteria were first shared with me twenty years ago by my friend and coaching colleague Rick Isaac of HR ChangeWorks. I have changed the two criteria somewhat, but the essential message Rick communicated to me is intact—the person who owns the goal and their manager must factor in time to 1) interact with each other during the goal pursuit and 2) re-evaluate goal progress at regular intervals.

» **S**pecific
» **M**easurable
» **A**ligned
» **R**ealistic
» **T**ime-bound
» **E**valuate
» **R**eadjust

SMARTER GOALS

Specific: Who is acting, what is happening, when is it happening, why is it happening, and how is it happening?

Measurable: What objective or subjective metrics—numeric or descriptive, quantitative or qualitative—will be used to determine when and if the goal is achieved?

Aligned: Does the goal contribute to achieving the goals of the organization, department, or team?

Realistic: Is this goal attainable within current or potential skills and capabilities?

Time-bound: When will the goal be achieved, or what is the frequency with which these actions will be carried out?

Evaluate: As the goal pursuit is occurring, ask: are the metrics providing meaningful, accurate, and useful information for action? After measurement has been completed, ask: what could have been improved or done even better or more effectively?

Readjust: Do the metrics need to change or adjust to new conditions? What needs to be done differently going forward? Should any new behaviors or actions be added?

In addition to bringing further precision and specificity to a statement about your destination, there is a more important reason for applying the "smarter" criteria. The process creates a two-way, ongoing conversation and alignment document between manager and individual/team that solidifies a shared understanding and agreement about what is being pursued.

ONE LETTER AT A TIME

The best way to apply "smarter" criteria to a draft goal is one letter at a time. Let's take our example with Jane once again.

> **Draft 2:** I will have an open mind that values all opinions and feedback from everyone I work with. I will solicit and welcome feedback, criticism, new ideas, and challenges as opportunities for me to learn. I will be known for openness, patience, and listening.

Is the goal Specific enough? Can we tell who is involved, who is accountable, what will happen, how it will happen, and why? Jane thought we could, and I agreed. One could argue it doesn't get specific enough regarding the "how," and that is a fair argument. We decided to tackle the "how" by explaining the specific tactics and actions linked to the goal.

Is it Measurable? What will determine if the goal has been achieved? This is always tricky when additional "soft skills" and new behaviors are key aspects of a goal and a subjective judgment of results is required. One way to address this is to focus on one or more observable events and behaviors. For example, feedback can be actively solicited from bosses, peers, and direct reports over a period of time. What do they observe? How do they describe changes in behaviors and approaches? What value do they place on the perceived changes? Can they quantify the perceived value on a scale of 1 to 7? We decided on some potential metrics and decided to revisit this criteria at the end of the smart review.

BEING SMART ABOUT SMARTER GOALS

A few words of caution on the "smarter" goal criteria:

1. In a business context, "smarter" goals can be effective for boosting numbers or solving customer complaints. But for grandiose goals—for anyone aspiring to do what he or she loves for a living, or someone who wants to be perceived as being open and nondefensive in all their interactions—the "smarter" goal methodology can get in the way of or hinder innovation.

2. "Smarter" goals aren't always that smart, especially for those aiming to achieve something really big.

3. Make sure the measurement(s) chosen for the developmental goal are appropriate. There are two primary types of metric: quantitative variables and attribute variables.

Quantitative Variables: The values of a quantitative variable can be ordered and measured. Examples include number of customer complaints, proportion of customers eligible for a rebate, fill weight of a product box to be shipped.

Attribute Variables: Attribute variables are also called categorical variables or qualitative variables. The values of an attribute variable can be put into a countable number of categories or different groups. Categorical data may or may not have some logical order. Examples include survey results (1 = Disagree, 2 = Neutral, 3 = Agree), payment method (cash or credit), machine settings (low, medium, high), and product types (wood, plastic, metal).

Use quantitative measures when goal progress can be measured in numbers or percentages. Use attributes when the goal will yield a qualitative result.

Is it Aligned? Does the goal contribute directly or indirectly to the strategic intent of the team, department/division, and organization? We confirmed the goal was relevant to the strategic intent of the organization and the business unit Jane belonged to. The key organizational initiative being embraced globally and locally was improving the quality and quantity of innovation in all facets of the business. Our challenge became how to link and align Jane's goal with the innovation initiative.

Is it Realistic? Can Jane accomplish it with some reasonable amount of certainty? We discussed this and determined it was definitely attainable and within reach, given discipline and practice.

Is the goal bound by Time? In the goal's second-draft form, this was not clear enough, so Jane and I wordsmithed the goal statement by adding a six-month timeframe to the goal.

After making changes based on this "smarter" criteria, the final destination came into sharper focus:

> **Final Goal Statement:** During the next six months, I will practice behaviors (e.g., empathy, listening, vulnerability) demonstrating I have an open mind that values all opinions and feedback from everyone I work with. I will proactively solicit feedback, criticism, new ideas, and challenges. I will value these viewpoints as opportunities for personal and professional growth and improvement. I will become known for my openness, patience, and listening.
>
> This goal will be measured over the course of six months by:
>
> » Three feedback sessions with my boss
> » Concluding 360-feedback comparisons (boss, peers, direct reports, indirect reports)
> » Use of coaching measurement scorecard (pp. 62–63) to track qualitative evaluations and quantitative results, including perceived and

COACHING SCORECARD

The "coaching measurement scorecard" being referred to was developed by my coaching colleagues at BPI group. I tailor and customize the tool for my coaching clients, but these talented people developed the framework. Mary Herrmann, managing director of the BPI group's global executive coaching practice, explains the tool this way:

> "One guarantee with every coaching assignment is the challenge of measuring results. All coaches soon come to the realization that measurement is both essential and difficult. BPI group's ROI Coaching Dashboard is a proprietary tool to help identify the tangible and intangible business impacts and benefits from a coaching project."

The measurement of the coaching you do as a manager is both essential and difficult. The scorecard tool can help you and the individual or team being coached to identify the qualitative and quantitative benefits of your coaching. A partial example of the tool appears on the facing page.

COACHING SCORECARD

Your Name:

	Measure	Impact ($ impact or Great/ Good/Opposite of Good)
Quantitative Benefits	Team Performance & Productivity	
	Quality (Product/Services)	
	Key Performance Indicators	
	Customer Service	
	Employee Engagement	
	Self-Motivation & Retention	
	Cost Reduction	
	Revenue Growth	
	Profitability	
	Team Morale	
	Other Business Impacts (specify)	

		Impact ($ impact or Great/ Good/Opposite of Good)
Qualitative Benefits	Relationship with Boss	
	Relationship with Peers	
	Relationship with Direct Reports	
	Improved Relationship with Indirect Reports	
	Enhanced Emotional Commitment (self)	
	Conflict Resolution	
	Improved Communication Skills	
	Improved Teamwork	
	Other Intangibles (specify)	

observable increases in the number and quality of creative ideas and innovations introduced

My longer-term goal is to turn these behaviors into reliable and sustainable habits to enhance my leadership brand at the company and increase the number of documented innovations introduced to internal and external customers.

Is Jane's goal perfect? No, of course not, and that is not the outcome we were after. The primary purpose is always this: the development goal must align with the strategy and goals of the organization and be largely written—and 100 percent owned—by the individual or team. You need to see tangible signs people are becoming emotionally committed and intrinsically motivated to achieve the goal. The individual or team must want to achieve the goal before they will be willing to practice new behaviors or actions.

Sometimes amidst the initial rush of emotional commitment to a new goal, the individual or team members being managed will get cold feet and become too careful about taking the risks necessary to achieve the outcomes desired. The opposite can occur as well. They become so excited they overdo it, and the new behaviors being cultivated are in danger of being perceived as so different that they are "over the top." In the next chapter, we'll focus on the common-sense pursuit of developmental goals and how a manager and coach can help people practice new behaviors and actions effectively.

Postscript: Jane made excellent progress on her smart development goal, and because she had metrics and an evaluation plan in place, she was able to Evaluate and Readjust as necessary during the six-month implementation.

BHAGs

Here's a concluding thought about "stretch goals," what are known as "big hairy audacious goals" (BHAGs)—an idea conceptualized in Jim Collins and Jerry I. Porras's book *Built to Last: Successful Habits of Visionary Companies.* On

November 21, 1963, the day before President Kennedy was shot and killed, he delivered a speech in San Antonio, Texas, in which he said:

> *Frank O'Connor, the Irish writer, tells in one of his books how, as a boy, he and his friends would make their way across the countryside, and when they came to an orchard wall that seemed too high and too doubtful to try and too difficult to permit their voyage to continue, they took off their hats and tossed them over the wall—and then they had no choice but to follow them.*
>
> *This Nation has tossed its cap over the wall of space, and we have no choice but to follow it. Whatever the difficulties, they will be overcome. Whatever the hazards, they must be guarded against…with the help of all those who labor in the space endeavor, with the help and support of all Americans, we will climb this wall with safety and with speed—and we shall then explore the wonders on the other side.*

President Kennedy knew bold goals and actions require risk and courage, and his speech in San Antonio likened America's publicly proclaimed goal of landing a man on the moon by the decade's end as analogous to "throwing our cap over the wall." When faced with the myriad business challenges leaders and managers confront, opting for bolder choices—the ones that make you slightly uncomfortable because you have never done them before—can be the best, and perhaps wisest, choice.

[▶]

DISCIPLINE 3 SUMMARY

Since the most effective and energizing type of motivation comes from within, goals must be developed and finalized by the individual or team being managed and coached. The individual or team must own and genuinely want to pursue and achieve the goals they align to the strategies of the organization. From the coaching perspective, one of the best ways to help people visualize and finalize goal statements is to follow these three steps:

1. Start with "what if?"
2. Write a draft of the desired destination, without restriction and inhibition
3. Align the destination with "smarter" criteria

And always keep in mind: fortune favors the bold—those willing to "strike another match and start anew."

ENERGIZERS

Here are some reinforcing and energizing ideas to consider when practicing Discipline 3: Align Destination.

If you want someone to set the right goals...

✅ Make "smart" goals SMARTER.

Most coaches know developmental goals should be SMART (specific, measurable, achievable, realistic, time-bound), but you can make them smarter by also "Evaluating" and "Readjusting" them. Developmental goals should not be set in stone and should change over time.

✅ Write goals that focus on strengths and opportunities, as well as on ending behaviors that get in the way.

Helping people identify the behaviors that require their attention is often the real art of managing and coaching. Focusing on strengths is good, but remember:

overfocusing on the positive ignores the research and practical wisdom that tell us it is *negative* behavior that derails careers. Top managers and coaches help people improve by first helping them stop behaviors getting in the way.

✅ *Ensure goals are relevant to organizational goals and priorities.*
Each goal needs to have meaning in the person's life. Be certain that the person you are managing and coaching considers not only what is most important to them but also the contribution to the team, department/division, and organization.

"Of all the things I have done, the most vital was coordinating the talents of those who work for me and pointing them at certain goals."
—Walt Disney

"It is good to have an end to journey toward; but it is the journey that matters, in the end."
—Ernest Hemingway

DISCIPLINE 4: TAKE ACTION

*"It doesn't matter whether you are pursuing
success in business, sports, the arts, or life in general:
The bridge between wishing and accomplishing is discipline."*
—Harvey Mackay

*"Success is a matter of understanding and religiously practicing
specific, simple habits that always lead to success."*
—Robert J. Ringer

*"Practice means to perform, over and over again in the face
of all obstacles, some act of vision, of faith, of desire.
Practice is a means of inviting the perfection desired."*
—Martha Graham

Charles Kettering once wrote: "A problem well-stated is a problem half-solved."
His message is a good one. If you can understand and, as objectively as possible,
describe "the problem," you will have taken an important step in the direction
of finding solutions. The same holds true for achieving a goal or arriving at

a desired destination. A goal well-stated is a goal half-achieved. The previous chapter described techniques to help develop and finalize a well-stated goal. Now you'll turn your attention to execution and goal achievement.

GOAL ACHIEVEMENT

When it comes to making progress and producing measurable results, there are two critical things you can influence as a manager and coach: the goal and the ability to take action. Once you have helped someone articulate and document a desired destination, your biggest challenge becomes overcoming barriers that prevent people from demonstrating behaviors and implementing actions at the level of excellence and quality required.

The achievement of development goals requires three sequential actions:

1. The discipline to practice new behaviors, tactics, and strategies
2. The willingness to evaluate progress and listen to feedback
3. The courage to readjust behaviors, tactics, metrics, strategies, and even the goal itself

The last two actions may sound familiar. They are how, in *Discipline 3,* we made SMART goals SMARTER: by *Evaluating* progress toward the goal and *Readjusting* to stay on target. The first action—the discipline to practice new behaviors, tactics, and strategies—is trickier. It requires a slightly adjusted coaching role for you: to apply an increasingly structured approach, and to encourage the appropriate mindset in the person or team you are managing, in which fear is eliminated and courage cultivated.

ADJUSTED ROLE FOR YOU

For the individuals or teams you manage, acquiring the discipline to effectively pursue a goal requires you, as manager, to introduce additional practice and structure. For example, in my coaching practice, I meet or talk with each client at agreed-upon, consistent intervals to ensure they remain focused on both the goal and the behaviors and/or actions needed to achieve it. It is important for you, as a manager, to establish a similar routine.

Tailor your approach and style to the current situation and to the individual or team you are managing. Yet, remember your primary role remains the same: to assist the person or team being managed in selecting the best options for goal achievement and to offer specific advice, direction, or correction only when necessary; that is, when an individual or team consistently gets stuck or lost.

Like goal identification, goal pursuit and achievement are infinitely more motivating when those accountable for the goal are able to draw conclusions for themselves. However, there can be no sugar-coated feedback on this rung. No one enjoys hearing bad news or difficult feedback, but we all need to, nevertheless. The person you are managing will not be able to create the best design, options, and strategies for practicing and achieving a goal unless they have your best advice and counsel: both positive and negative.

Once, after I missed a deadline for a client deliverable, one of the best coaching managers I ever had told me: "I'm going to make it extremely uncomfortable for you because of this mistake, but the good news is I'm going to coach you so you won't do it again." He was correct. I'm glad he talked straight and didn't back away from a tough message when I needed it. During the next three months, he coached and taught me unforgettable and timeless lessons about project management I use to this day.

To talk straight as a coaching manager, you must remain neutral—impartial and unbiased—in order to help those you are managing to clearly see options and possible paths. This does not mean you should ignore your accountability as a manager. Your organization will always rely on you to be protective of organizational assets and willing to represent the interests of the organization with your own good name. Being a coaching manager helps you do this—by strengthening the bond of trust and your relationship with your people, you are strengthening the emotional commitment they have in you and in the organization.

One of the best stories to help explain the impartial role of the coaching manager on this rung comes from an ancient Sufi riddle, first told by Hazrat Ali, Mohammed's son-in-law, in Arabia around 750 AD. A version of it is related on Arthur Lau's "Jadeite Jade" website.

See if you can solve this timeless riddle and understand its application to managing.

A Sufi master was near death. He knew his three disciples had yet to learn the great truth and way of the Sufis. He wanted to make sure that, upon his death, the three disciples would be able to come under the tutelage and guidance of another Sufi master.

The Sufi master owned seventeen camels. He made a bequest with an instruction his disciples had to follow strictly:

"The three of you shall divide the camels in the following proportions: the eldest disciple shall have half, the one in the middle shall have one-third, while the youngest shall have one-ninth."

He died after his bequest was written.

Now the three disciples were in a dilemma. The master's instructions were oblique, because seventeen is a number that can't be divided at all, except by itself. So, the three disciples sought advice from learned men on how to divide the seventeen camels.

Someone told them to own the camels communally, and when the camels reproduced they might be able to find a suitable solution. Someone else told them to make the nearest possible division. An old, wise trader said they should sell the camels and divide the proceeds. A local judge asserted the bequest was legally null and void because it could not be executed at all.

As the three disciples had been under the guidance of the old Sufi master for some years, they had achieved some aptitude for thinking wisely. Thus, they knew their master might have inserted some hidden wisdom in his bequest. They made further enquiries as to whom they could consult in order to arrive at a satisfactory answer to this seemingly insoluble problem.

An old trader in the market said he could not see the answer to their problem, but he knew someone who would be able to help them: Hazrat Ali. Hazrat Ali listened to the conundrum, asked a few questions, and came up with an idea:

"I can add my camel to the flock, and that will make the total number of camels eighteen. The eldest disciple shall have one-half, and that will be nine. The middle disciple shall have one-third, and that will be six. The youngest disciple shall have one-ninth and that will be two. One camel will then be left over, and it will be returned to me."

And that was how the three disciples found their new Sufi master.

How is Hazrat Ali's role in the story similar to a manager's? First, he is a neutral and impartial observer. He has no stake in the outcome, yet he comes to fully understand the issue and its associated stumbling blocks. Next, he sees the disciples are hopelessly stuck, and he wants to help. He decides to share an idea that could help the disciples find a way out of their dilemma. This is very similar to the role of the manager in many, although not all, situations.

When an individual or team is truly stuck, don't let them dangle in the wind. Yes, a manager must avoid stepping in with answers too quickly. But you also have a unique external perspective on what the individual or team is struggling with. It is perfectly fine to share that point of view when required.

To solve the riddle, the disciples had to go beyond the normal, taken-for-granted, obvious, and easy routes. They had trouble doing this in part because they had difficulty stepping back from the situation to get a new perspective. The disciples were looking for, and even committed to getting, something from this situation: their shares of their master's assets. The thought that they had to add something or give something up did not even enter their minds, nor those of the tradition-bound experts and gurus they first approached.

STRUCTURED APPROACH

One of the more effective structured approaches to practicing new behaviors and achieving goals is GROW. The model originated in the United Kingdom and was developed by Graham Alexander, Alan Fine, and Sir John Whitmore. GROW stands for Goal, Reality, Options, and Will (or Way Forward). (One excellent description is found in Max Landsberg's book *The Tao of Coaching*.)

The GROW model can be merged with another effective structured approach to discovering the best actions for a given situation: SWOT Analysis. SWOT is an acronym for Strengths, Weaknesses, Opportunities, and Threats.

GROW	SWOT Questions
Goal	» Look at the goal statement and ask: What new behaviors will be required to achieve the goal? » What strengths do I possess that will help me achieve the goal? » What do I need to improve or strengthen before taking action to achieve the goal?

Reality	» What is the current situation or context for practicing and achieving the goal?
	  » What opportunities exist today that will help achieve the goal? Driving factors)
	  » What threats exist that will be obstacles to goal practice and achievement? (Resisting factors)
	» What behaviors or actions need to be avoided?
	» What level of support do I need from people who could be affected by my goal practice and achievement?

Options	» What are the options available for taking action or changing behavior? » What criteria can be used to select the best of these options?
Will	» What are the risks and threats to, and benefits of, implementation? » What commitments must be made to take action and make progress? » How can I start? What moves me (or us) in the right direction?

SWOT Analysis is a simple but useful framework for identifying these character-istics inherent in a project or business. It involves specifying a project or business goal and then identifying the internal and external factors that support or miti-gate against achieving the goal.

The SWOT framework on p. 74 shows how to combine with the GROW model to help the individuals you manage crystallize the discipline and new behaviors needed to work on their development goals.

The appropriate mindset. Here are four strategies to help those you are managing and coaching solidify the right mindset and gain the courage to achieve their development goals by practicing new behaviors.

STRATEGY 1: HELP PUSH OUT FEAR

Often the toughest obstacle to practicing a new behavior or taking proactive steps to achieve a developmental goal is fear: Fear of failure. Fear that others will react negatively. Fear of vulnerability and embarrassing yourself.

You must provide the support to make practice as safe as possible. Start with small steps and feedback metrics. New actions and behaviors that support developmental goals demand patience and supportive guidance from coaching managers. Applaud the practice, talk objectively about the results, and encourage the use of metrics.

Mistakes are common during practice, and for good reason. Making mistakes is a crucial step in learning and improving. Your role is to ensure teams and individuals feel secure about identifying errors and learning from them. Make sure they are aware that, the more challenging the goal, the more frequent and difficult setbacks will be. That's okay.

When I'm managing someone who I know or suspect has fears about practicing a new behavior, I apply these tactics and emphasize the importance of preparation. If a moment of actual crisis occurs, I want the people I manage and coach to be able to fall back on plans made in a calm state rather than give in to the cortisol-and-adrenaline-infused fight-or-flight response of the moment. The right amount of preparation—balancing the need for control and the need for spontaneity—is rational, and thinking ahead to mitigate the damage of a mistake can often be the best protection against the unexpected.

Here are three techniques for any coaching manager to help overcome debilitating fears.

Journaling

For the individual(s) or team(s) you manage, this is a healthy process at any time, but especially after goals are finalized. The pursuit of a goal often requires taking steps outside one's comfort zone. Writing helps organize thinking, and organized thinking can help instill the confidence to act. Typically, after a goal is established, the mind swirls with thoughts, ideas, tasks, and worries. Even people who have little or no trouble staying focused can find it hard to manage so many thoughts at once.

Writing down ideas, or graphically imagining possible actions directed toward a goal, can provide plans and images that build the confidence to pursue it. Writing also brings fear into focus, giving both you and your employees greater awareness of the fear's causes.

Perspective.

By helping your people put negative thoughts and feelings in perspective, you can help them learn to deal with fear constructively. You have probably noticed some people you manage tend to focus too much on the negative—especially when receiving feedback. Feedback's value lies in how you use it to improve, not how it makes the recipient feel. Remind the person you are managing of this. To provide perspective during the pursuit of a goal, I like to ask at least twice: *What's the worst that can happen?* Really, what is the *worst* that can happen?

Understand "Failure"

Bob Dylan once wrote: "There's no success like failure. And failure is no success at all." This often-quoted line is not some fatuous sidebar. It can be interpreted as a plea to treat failure as any great scientist would: failure is a data point for learning and a stepping stone to success.

For far too many of the people you will manage, failure feels like it defines who they are as a person. Society, parents, friends, colleagues, and even internal thoughts have all—at one time or another—conspired to twist the meaning of specific events in all of our lives:

» Failing an exam means you're not smart enough.
» Failing to get trim and fit means you're undesirable.
» Failing in business means you don't have what it takes.
» Failing at art means you're not creative. And so on.

To the scientist, a negative result is not an indication they are bad at what they do. In fact, quite the opposite is true. Proving a hypothesis wrong is often just as useful as proving it right, because you have learned something along the way.

We all must learn: failures are data points that can help lead you to the right answer. Failure is essentially the cost you pay to get it right. None of this is to say you should try to make mistakes on purpose or that failing is fun. Certainly, some failures can lead to disastrous results.

But failure will always be part of growth for those being managed and coached, for one simple reason: when someone is focused on building a new habit, learning a new skill, or mastering a craft of any kind, they are experimenting. If you run enough experiments, you're going to get a "negative result" at times.

This happens to every scientist and will continue to happen to you, me, and whomever you are managing. Sometimes, the result of an action taken in pursuit of a goal can be perceived negatively by the person who takes the action, but quite positively by others.

STRATEGY 2: HELP COMMUNICATE AND SOCIALIZE GOALS

One of the big mistakes people make in communicating a goal is they don't "socialize" it. "Socialize" in this context means to connect the goal with the interests of the people who can either help you achieve it or hinder your progress.

I once coached the chief HR officer at a Fortune 500 company, who had drafted a goal to identify, develop, and implement an "HR scorecard" process to track critical people-related metrics. The executive and his team crafted a beautifully clear PowerPoint presentation explaining the scorecard's purpose, as well as a communication plan to increase awareness, support, and buy-in for developing and implementing the process, which involved using the digital scorecard to help manage people across various business units. After several weeks of near-flawless presentations and meetings, the HR team sensed trouble in getting other division heads interested.

"I don't know," explained the HR head at our first meeting. "We see a lot of heads nodding 'yes' at these scorecard meetings, but there's no action on their part to help out or contribute ideas. And we've socialized the heck out of this." I asked a few questions and took a look at the presentation and communication materials. It was clear to me what this leader meant by "socialization" and what I meant were quite different. I saw no clear, direct connection between the goal being proposed—to create a digitized HR/people scorecard for the company— and the value-add for each of the respective divisions and business units. The dots were not being connected, and I wasn't even sure the HR team working on the project was aware of all the dots that needed connecting.

As I got involved with the HR head and his team, I asked if they would consider adding a section to their scorecard template: Value to the Business. I gave them a few examples to clarify my suggestion. I wanted them to tailor the scorecard metrics to the quantitative metrics each of the divisions and business units were rightly obsessed with, such as market share growth, cost, productivity, and margins. The team developed metrics, as shown on pp. 80–81.

Next, the team developed case-study scenarios to quantify the benefits of tracking *and* improving these metrics by 5, 10, and 20 percent. We then talked about making another attempt at socializing the scorecard, enlisting support in implementing the process, and achieving the anticipated value. The communication plan was altered to gain support and buy-in first from the head of each division and business unit, and, once that was secured, to have further meetings with the VPs and directors. The focus of all the meetings was on adding new value and insight to their respective business lines.

There was a big difference between these meetings and the earlier ones that had so puzzled the HR head. The main difference was the division and business-unit executive leaders were engaged and excited about how the scorecard could help them manage *their* businesses. While the scorecard continues to be refined and improved, the catalyst for the initiative's success was socializing the HR leader's goal to the business value perceived by each of the different business groups in the organization.

STRATEGY 3: HELP CREATE AN ACTION PLAN

Once someone has fully committed to achieving a developmental goal, your role shifts to helping with action planning. One of the biggest problems preventing individuals and teams from accomplishing their big goals and aspirations is they don't think small enough.

The reason for thinking small is simple. You need momentum, and nothing builds momentum like focusing on a few small steps and checking off a few accomplishments. The purpose of these smaller actions is not only to get people closer to their goal, but to work on strengthening belief and discipline skills.

Action planning has as much to do with strengthening positive habits as with breaking a goal down into actionable steps. A written plan is, after all, just a piece of paper; it lacks discipline. Again, the three most important words to remember when practicing the discipline to achieve goals are: Focus. Focus. Focus. This near obsessive focus must be on small, practical steps that will get you where you want to go.

TALENT QUALITY INDEX

METRIC: QUALITY OF HIRE

Formula: Survey to hiring manager at new hire 90 days. Performance evaluation score correlated with hiring effectiveness at 1-year mark

Value to the Business: Allows us to reduce "mismatches" due to miscommunication and fine-tune recruiting services to hiring managers. Better selection that more closely matches business needs to increase productivity and reduce turnover.

METRIC: COST PER HIRE

Formula: Total hiring costs × 1.1 factor ÷ total hires

Value to the Business: Measures the "effectiveness" of recruiting from a financial perspective. As we become more efficient in attracting and selecting top talent, the cost of recruiting can be reduced and our margins can be increased.

METRIC: TIME TO HIRE

Formula: Days from approved requisition date to employee start date

Value to the Business: This is an "efficiency" number. Decreasing the number of days to fill open requisitions will increase productivity and improve the talent pool.

PEOPLE RETENTION INDEX

HIGH PERFORMER RETENTION

Formula: 1 minus high performers in key positions who leave ÷ all high performers in key positions

Value to the Business: This will identify the "retention rate" (positive side of turnover) of high performers in key positions. Cost of losing key people is directly related to margins, productivity, and market-share.

TURNOVER

Formula 1: Total separations ÷ regular headcount
Value to the Business: Total turnover looks at the dollar cost of separations. "Very low" turnover might indicate under-performers remaining on payroll and "very high" turnover indicates wasted cost in replacement.

Formula 2: Voluntary separations ÷ regular headcount
Value to the Business: Voluntary separation is an indicator of poor "recruitment" in management practices that negatively impact market-share (officers taking books of business with them), margin (excess expense over an "acceptable rate"), and productivity (negative effects on work teams).

Formula 3: Involuntary separations ÷ regular headcount
Value to the Business: Involuntary separations (terminations for cause and some RIFs) show the level of ineffectiveness in staffing decisions, as well as performance management practices. Ultimately, high involuntary separations are costly.

The experience of progress is more important than absolute clarity of goals when it comes to team members feeling positive about a project, and ultimately doing their best work. It makes sense to incorporate multiple milestones, break a goal down within the workplan of a project, and focus on ensuring team members experience a sense of progress.

Let's say your long-term goal is to be recognized as the manager with the best coaching skills in your entire organization. Your three-year goal is to become a role model when it comes to coaching teams, individuals, and even other coaches. A lofty and worthwhile goal, and maybe even achievable in three years. But how will you do this?

Start by breaking the goal down into smaller actions by using the "and how?" technique. For example:

» Develop my own unique point of view about what coaching is and what it does. And how?
  » Get referrals to the three best coaching books and three best coaching articles. Read them all.
  » Write my own personal philosophy statement about coaching.
» Practice something all great coaches do exceptionally well. And how?
  » Practice providing feedback. Don't hold back and talk straight.
  » Practice asking interesting, open-ended questions. And how?
    » Ask questions when you are genuinely curious about the answer.
    » Ask questions to make people think, yet don't put them on the defensive.
» Build trust and confidence in my coaching abilities. And how?
  » Ask for confidential feedback.
  » Focus on strengthening ETC (Empathy, Trust, Commitment).

Each action step should have a timeframe attached to it. You might find yourself working on multiple actions concurrently or knocking them out sequentially, one after another. Either way is fine; the trick is to ensure you stay on track by keeping your actions in a timeframe.

STRATEGY 4: HELP SUSTAIN INSPIRATION

A "tell" in poker is a change in behavior or demeanor providing clues to a player's assessment of their hand. A player gains an advantage if they observe and understand the meaning of another player's "tell," particularly if it is unconscious and reliable.

There is a not-so-subtle "tell" from managers and coaches in need of inspiration: they speak of their organization, their team, or their lives in the past tense, never the present or future. Whenever I notice this, I sit up and pay attention, because people who can't imagine their situations in the present tense are already in trouble. This "tell" reveals something particularly dangerous and potentially destructive because, to paraphrase the late RAND economist Charles Wolf, Jr., self-defeating language portrays a past that wasn't, a present that isn't, and a future that probably won't be.

Having goals does not necessarily guarantee success or inspiration, but, as noted earlier, the odds of success can be increased if goal achievement is directly connected to an honest assessment of the past and present, as well as what is most important in the desired future. A person is intrinsically motivated to go after a goal if the desire for change comes from within—if the goal ignites internal energy and the passion to go for it. The manager's role, after a goal is written down and is being pursued, is to ask periodically: Why did you write this goal to begin with? Why is this goal still worthwhile?

It is often true halfway into pursuing a goal, the wind goes out of people's sails and they let it languish. That is the time for the coaching manager to help people dig a little deeper and renew the inspiration and vision that originally created the goal.

TAKE A BREAK

I recently coached a leader in the auto industry who had developed a lofty and worthwhile developmental goal but was in danger of losing his energy and commitment to it. Following is the goal he originally conceived along with the desired outcomes.

Goal: Add to my leadership brand by being known as a market and industry visionary viewed by executives as a leader among peers and someone who welcomes and faces up to difficult people or business decisions.

When achieved, this will result in:

» Positive perceptions about being a team player focused on constructively resolving conflict and doing what is best for the company

> » An increase in peers approaching me for advice and assistance with their challenges
> » New characteristics being added to my "leadership brand" (e.g., visionary, decisive, "gravitas," and confidence)
> » A perception of me as a multiskilled executive who continues to collaborate and who can fill a variety of executive roles within the company

Measurement of Progress: feedback from boss, peers, and direct reports; concluding 360-feedback comparisons; use of "coaching measurement scorecard" to track qualitative and quantitative results.

I could tell after about six weeks of following this action plan, the leader was losing enthusiasm and momentum. He still wanted to achieve the goal, but the day-to-day operational grind of his job was dulling positive perceptions of progress. He needed help, so we brainstormed a list of ideas on the whiteboard in his office. These are the ideas he thought were best.

» Take a brief goal break. For the next three weeks don't focus on actions that support the goal. Focus on operations, customers, and staff.
» For the next three months delegate 20 percent of day-to-day activities to direct reports in order to free up time to address current and unforeseen operational challenges.

» Take two ten-minute breaks every Monday, Wednesday, and Friday to re-evaluate the original goal statement. Ask these questions:
  » Why did I select this goal in the first place?
  » Why do I want to achieve this goal?
  » What will be the outcome for me, my team, and the organization when I achieve the goal?
» A pause in pursuit of this goal is not failure. A pause is…just a pause. Take as long as needed to refresh and regain perspective and energy. Keep boss in loop.

The intent of the brainstorming exercise was to address loss of momentum head-on. When the action plan with milestones and timelines became just a set of instructions or tasks, it created a feeling of dependence, of being controlled by someone or something else.

But when this executive understood he retained the authority to set the pace and to question and re-evaluate the plan—his plan—he began rediscovering the missing sense of independence. Furthermore, since the "blues" he was feeling emanated from this feeling of dependence, his energy would return if he could increase his level of independence and control over the goal. In fact, his energy did return once he had implemented the actions from the whiteboard brainstorming.

CASE STUDY: PRACTICING A NEW BEHAVIOR

Stephen Liu was a CIO at a Fortune 300 company whom I was coaching a few years ago, and he provides a good example of someone who developed and practiced a new behavior using all four of these strategies.

Stephen is one of the most disciplined managers and leaders I have ever met: always well prepared; a problem solver who is focused and highly organized. He came up through the IT ranks with an in-depth knowledge of infrastructure and a laser focus on customer requirements.

After completing a series of 360-feedback interviews and an online survey of his management team, I drafted a report for him to consider. It listed three strengths commonly perceived by his boss, peers, and direct and indirect reports:

1. Technical IT excellence
2. Work standards and accountability
3. Problem-solving skills

Two clear areas for improvement emerged:

1. Listening

Comments:

» "He can be ahead of us sometimes and needs to slow down, hear us, and help us catch up."
» "His determination and strong sense of vision sometimes prevent him from listening to others."
» "He defends his positions to the 'nth degree.'"

2. Leadership versatility

Comments:

» "Can be very black and white—has low tolerance for ambiguity."
» "Most comfortable using a directive style and doesn't often stray from that."
» "Hard to get to know. Lets people into his head but not his heart."

When I shared the results of this confidential 360-degree feedback, it was this last comment that captured Stephen's attention and animated him most. "People know me. They know what I stand for and how dedicated I am. I have a vision and I encourage everyone to join in and add to the vision. And I have a big heart, too. I want people to be happy here and as committed as I am to our vision and goals," he explained, a little perplexed by the comments about his lack of "leadership versatility."

I said my sense was, while people admired and respected him for his technical and problem-solving skills, they didn't feel they really knew him as a person. Had he ever shared any personal stories with his team, such as how he came to the United States from China or what his passion outside of work is? From this conversation, we both concluded he was very guarded about these topics at work and didn't really think they mattered that much in terms of getting results.

They matter a great deal, I remember saying to him. They matter because your ability or inability to connect with people at work on a human-to-human level will impact the *psychological safety* of individuals on your team and their level of *emotional commitment*—to you, to the company, to customers, and to the work itself. On the best teams, members listen to one another, share personal stories, see vulnerability as a strength, and back each other up, no matter what may come.

A team leader helps create an environment where it is safe to speak openly and freely—about anything—because the group will always have your back. A safety net is always there to catch someone taking a risk before they get hurt or inadvertently hurt others. The leader not only has to participate in creating a psychologically safe environment, but must act as its protector. It all starts, I told Stephen, with sharing some of your personal life stories and demonstrating vulnerability to the people you work with.

Stephen listened and uttered the three-letter word that brings music to the ears of any coach: "How?" I smiled and simply said, "I'm glad you asked."

More than one hundred fifty people reported to Stephen directly or indirectly. He felt it was impossible and impractical to forge a personal relationship with each one. (This was the first of many roadblocks Stephen would put in our path. This was not intentional. He was cautious by nature, examined things from every angle, and preferred to eliminate the reasons why something shouldn't be done before acting.) "You don't have to," I said to him. "Start with letting them get to know you. Do you have any meetings or big events coming up where most or all of your team will attend?"

Stephen replied that in about three weeks there was an IT Division "all-hands" meeting to which every member of his team was invited. About sixty people would participate in person and another one hundred or so from around the world would participate by live web videoconference. "What can you share about yourself at this event no one else in the audience knows?" I asked. Silence. So I asked again. More silence.

From our earlier discussion, I knew Stephen recognized the value of sharing something personal, but he was hesitant and stuck. So I asked something different. "Tell me about your recent trip to China. I remember at our last meeting you said you were going to China to visit with the developers and to visit with family. What went on? How was the personal side of the trip?"

"I went to see my mom. Probably for the last time. She is old and very sick." As we talked, I learned how inspiring his mom was to him. She raised him as a single mother and encouraged his education and interest in technology. She also instilled a love of literature—the classics from Dickens and Joyce to Faulkner and Hemingway—to counterbalance and complement his mechanical and technical talents.

"Let me guess," I said, "no one on your team knows this about you, right?" He nodded, indicating no one did. "Well, they must," I responded. "They are anxiously waiting for this. They genuinely want to get to know you better. A leader excels at sharing personal stories that make human-to-human contact real and genuine. That's part of the reason they are able to make such deep connections with people and to inspire teams and individuals." Stephen nodded again, this time in agreement. Once again he asked, "How?" "Share a personal story," I said. "Tell it at the all-hands meeting."

Personal Communication

Over the next couple of weeks, we exchanged emails about the opening speech Stephen was writing for the meeting. I had only three guidelines for him:

1. It has to be real.
2. It has to be personal and from the heart.
3. It has to be different from any other speech you have made to this audience. It should be legendary.

On the morning of the all-hands meeting, I arrived and sat in the back of the room. Stephen walked to the front holding a book. He looked at the sixty-plus people in the room and the video cameras carrying his image to one hundred more in countries around the world. He opened the book to page one, and then he spoke:

"'It was the best of times, it was the worst of times, it was the age of wisdom, it was the age of foolishness…it was the season of Light, it was the season of Darkness, it was the spring of hope, it was the winter of despair, we had everything before us, we had nothing before us…'"

"Why am I reading this to you now? I think it's true for us in IT today. All of us, including me. There are some things going well—we can point to projects that are on-time, on-budget, and delighting our internal customers. But there are other things not going very well.

"I know you are working long hours. I know we have processes, policies, procedures that are annoying and confusing. There are many obstacles—needless, valueless barriers—that get in your way every day at this organization. Some of you struggle to keep up. Some of you struggle with your manager. And some of you struggle with me and my behavior. I'm committed to doing something about all of these things and can make this promise: things will get better.

"Many of you know I was in China last month visiting our teams there. What you don't know is I was also visiting my mother. When I saw her, she looked very old to me and very frail. She is the one who encouraged me to read, study, and travel. In short, to follow my dreams. I read to you a few minutes ago from one of her books—*A Tale of Two Cities.* Those words are from the first page of the Charles Dickens classic. And this is the book she used to read to me when I was a young boy learning to speak English.

"My mother passed away two days ago. I'm glad I saw her last month and I'm grateful for the final talks we had. Let me also say there is no place I would rather be right now than with all of you.

NEVER COACH ON AN EMPTY STOMACH

Because in this 'worst of times' for me, it is also 'the best of times' to be surrounded by this team.

"I look forward to a great Q1 all-hands event this morning and a wonderful year ahead with all of you. Our next speaker is…"

Before Stephen could utter the next speaker's name, a roar of applause and emotion swept over the room. I can't say what was happening in the other locations, but from my vantage point at the back of the room, the feelings ranged from stunned to supportive and back to stunned again. The speech was legendary in its personal touch and dramatically different from Stephen's prior quarterly introductions. It took five full minutes for everyone to compose themselves and the next speaker to begin.

When I finally connected with Stephen during lunch that day, he was still being surrounded by people who wanted to shake his hand and let him know they were there for him. That's all I did, as well. I shook his hand and let him know I was always there for him.

DISCIPLINE 4 SUMMARY

The achievement of developmental goals requires three sequential actions:

1. The discipline to practice new behaviors, tactics, and strategies
2. The willingness to evaluate progress and listen to feedback
3. The courage to readjust behaviors, tactics, metrics, strategies, and even the goal itself

Acquiring the discipline to effectively pursue a goal requires you to introduce additional structure. As a manager who also coaches, you can combine the SWOT framework with the GROW model to help people solidify the discipline and new behaviors required to work on established developmental goals.

Here are four strategies to help the people and teams you manage develop the right mindset and the courage to achieve their developmental goals and get results by practicing new behaviors:

Strategy 1: Help push out fear

Strategy 2: Help communicate and socialize goals

Strategy 3: Help create an action plan

Strategy 4: Help sustain inspiration

ENERGIZERS

Here are some reinforcing and energizing ideas to consider when practicing Discipline 4: Take Action.

If you want someone to sustain success...

Provide a safety net of support. Make practice as safe as possible.
Start with small steps and feedback metrics. New actions and behaviors in support of developmental goals require patience and supportive guidance from coaching managers. Research has shown it takes twenty-one days to form a habit! Applaud the practice, talk objectively about the results, and encourage the use of metrics.

Maximize rewards. Minimize punishment.
Mistakes are common during practice, and for good reason. Making mistakes is a crucial step in learning and improving. Ensure people feel good about identifying an error and learning from it. Make sure they are aware that the more

challenging the goal, the more frequent and difficult setbacks will be...and that's okay.

✅ *Ask questions to help people learn from mistakes or missteps.*
Don't let someone fall into the trap of equating making mistakes with being a mistake. The mistake cannot be changed, but everyone has a choice about how to respond. Consider asking these questions after taking action or practicing a new behavior: What could have been done to avoid the mistake? What small mistakes, in sequence, contributed to the bigger mistake? Are there alternatives you should have considered? What changes are required to avoid making this mistake again? How do you think your behavior should/would change if you were in a similar situation again?

*"For the things we have to learn before we can do them,
we learn by doing them."*
—Aristotle

*"A coach is someone who can give correction
without causing resentment."*
—John Wooden

DISCIPLINE 5: PURSUE MASTERY

"One can have no smaller or greater mastery than mastery of oneself."
—Leonardo da Vinci

*"Confidence comes with mastery, and the combination
enables me to reach new heights."*
—Pauline Brown

"Learn the rules like a pro, so you can break them like an artist."
—Pablo Picasso

When asked how he created his statue of David, Michelangelo is reported to have said, "It was easy. You just chip away the stone that doesn't look like David. David was in there, and I just had to find him." Chiseling something as near-divinely perfect as the David in Florence, Italy, is not what you are aiming for in this final rung.

The *pursuit* of "a David" is what you are after. The diligent and persistent pursuit of mastery is the goal, and continuous learning and improvement are the by-products that keep on giving...to the people you manage, to your organization, and to yourself.

If you have been a manager longer than a week, you know the role is often a series of adventures or misadventures. Adventures by their very nature involve uncertainty, risk, and often pain. But they also bring the possibility of reward and the fulfillment that accompanies the quest for your own forms of success.

Research from Malcolm Gladwell and others suggests 10,000 hours of practice are required to achieve the level of mastery associated with being a "world-class expert" in anything. In countless studies of accomplished composers, basketball players, concert pianists, chess players, and other professionals, the 10,000-hour figure comes up again and again. However, the 10,000 hours of practice needed for you or those you manage to achieve mastery is not the goal. The goal is the never-ending *pursuit of mastery.*

There is an inner sense in most managers I have met that mastery of something—anything—is actually unattainable. "Mastery" is an idealist's foolish concept of perfection. Those who earn the "master" brand or reputation are really just farther along the path, more advanced in their successes, failures, and skills than what we commonly observe.

What are the attitudes and behaviors essential to the pursuit of mastery in managing and coaching? To answer this question, I suggest you think about the best manager or coach you ever had. The best ones I had shared two attributes: they had remarkable insight into both my strengths and weaknesses, and they were relentless in their pursuit of helping me improve. "Relentless" may be the key word:

» Relentless in helping me face myself
» Relentless in helping me understand what I needed to do differently
» Relentless in keeping me on track

» Relentless in offering ideas when I was stuck

» Relentless in their support of and confidence in me

It is difficult to change habits and old ways of doing things. A coaching manager can help someone make the changes necessary, for example, to improve work relationships, achieve goals and targets, and strengthen their professional brand.

Have you ever decided to improve your communication skills, collaborate more with peers, work within a multigenerational team, read the *Wall Street Journal* every morning, or even get in a consistent six to eight hours of sleep every night? Perhaps you made it through the first few days of following through on such decisions. But then, as the days passed by, all your good intentions mysteriously started fading away, your habit-changing efforts stopped, and you were left disappointed, angry with yourself, and confused about what went awry.

After going through this pattern a couple of times, it's easy to get discouraged. The same thing can happen to the people you manage. As you back off from the structure and one-on-one time so critical during *Discipline 4: Take Action,* old behaviors can start creeping back into day-to-day interactions. It's hard to discern this pattern in a given week or two, but after a month or so it becomes clear that the new developmental goals and habits may lack staying power.

In the finite world of business, everything ultimately pushes up against a constraint. In the managing world, that constraint involves *sustainability.* How can you help your team members sustain a new behavior or new professional brand when you, the coaching manager, are no longer around or consistently available? Signs that sustainability is weakening must not be ignored.

Typically, falling back into old behaviors takes one of two forms: the "Kabuki effect" and the "human condition" or human nature.

Kabuki—the ancient Japanese theater-art form in which actors employ masks, makeup, and illusion—is a metaphor for managing and coaching that involves stylized, convincing, but ultimately meaningless posturing. Lack of sustainability once a coaching manager backs off can show up in many ways, depending on the original developmental goal:

» The listening skills, practiced so diligently and carefully during *Disciplines 2, 3, and 4* begin to give way to the old previously preferred "telling" style of "my way or the highway."

» A relentless focus on time-management skills and high-priority items dissolves into the style of the past: disorganized and constantly late.

» New collaboration behaviors with peers revert to unproductive competition and defensive positioning.

The new way of doing things may have been just a long, drawn-out Kabuki drama. The Kabuki effect may occur when, right from the start, the person being managed was never really serious enough about owning and implementing the new or revised steps and learnings. Instead, the manager discovers the person has been proposing goals they would never actually implement over the long haul.

The illusory nature of this Kabuki dance with the manager should have been evident from the start, but often it is not, either because the person being managed is good at "faking it" or the manager is so serious and self-absorbed in their own questions and suggestions that they don't see the signs. Obviously, this goes against one of the first principles of managing and coaching success: there must be sincere trust and effort from both the manager and the individual being managed.

What follows is a brief story about a master Kabuki dancer I ran into during one of my early coaching experiences. It was not a pleasant outcome for either of us. I'm often asked if I have experienced any "failures" in being a coach. In a word, yes. And Ray Dancer remains my prime example. (Just to be clear: this is a fictitious name.)

When I first met Ray, he was a vociferous champion of abstaining from any "new" management techniques that came after Frederick Taylor's 1911 book

The Principles of Scientific Management. But, then, no one is perfect, I thought. His idea of "self-managed work teams" or an "agile" or "scrum process" on the production floor was when someone brought him his favorite cup of black coffee. In short, he loved all ideas, as long as they were his own.

But during the first four months of coaching, Ray would extol, in the most eloquent words, the value he was receiving from coaching and how much his errant management ways had changed. And he really did change. He started listening to his production staff and the engineers who reported to him. He was getting along much better with his boss and collaborating with peers. The concluding 360-feedback report was like night and day compared to the 360 done when he began to get coaching.

You know what's coming: toward the end of the coaching process, I have never seen anyone snap back so quickly into the worst of their human motivations or display such an overabundance of self-serving blather and blistering critiques of their boss, direct reports, and coach. Ray was the best Kabuki dancer I have ever seen. He danced the dance around me and everyone he worked with during the structured coaching process. As soon as that structure was relaxed, he was back to his old habits and ways of thinking. He was "transitioned out" of his company within four months after the end of my "coaching."

I've drawn a caricature portrait of Ray, and that's not completely fair. A recurrent theme in my coaching work is never to belittle, demean, or judge anyone too harshly, if at all. I don't know for certain what they may have lived through or what their life story is all about. Ray's wife had been in a car accident and had suddenly become a quadriplegic several years before I met him. He was caring for her whenever he wasn't at work. About a year before I met him, he had turned sixty-two and qualified for his company's defined-benefit retirement plan. I'm not saying any of these facts excused his sometimes belligerent and prickly nature at work. But I think the way they might have driven or influenced his behavior should be factored in.

If you are truly seeking to help someone cement positive habits and pursue mastery, it would be a good idea to get a sense—if you haven't already done so—of the challenges in that person's life. Wouldn't it be a good test of this relationship of trust if the person you were managing and coaching felt comfortable sharing details about the fastballs, knuckleballs, and curves life has thrown their way?

I sometimes share a work-life integration wheel with my coaching clients. This gives them a way to self-assess the factors that influence and shape balance and perspective in their lives. The wheel can provide a quick snapshot or overview of the aspects of a person's life that are going well or not going well.

The second form of falling back into old behaviors occurs because, well, we are human, not the unemotional decision makers depicted in most economics textbooks. Quite the opposite. We often choose immediate rewards over greater future benefits. We take the path of least resistance, typically by going with the status quo or simply not taking action.

Take the act of coaching. Managers know it's important, yet many haven't devoted enough time or practice to improving their coaching skills. Why? Enter behavioral economics and an apt analogy: saving for retirement. Again, we all know it's important, but studies, tables, and graphs have shown many people have not done a good job of it. For decades, employees were cajoled, hit with sticks, and teased with carrots to participate in retirement savings plans. But human inertia often won out and, even with generous matching contributions, many employees stayed away.

Then employers, with the blessing of changed governance rules, began to automatically enroll employees in savings plans. People could opt out, but good old human inertia—now having changed sides and working in favor of automatic enrollment—stopped many from doing so.

Vanguard, an investment firm that administers retirement savings plans for employers, discovered the default decisions made by plan sponsors under

WORK-LIFE INTEGRATION WHEEL

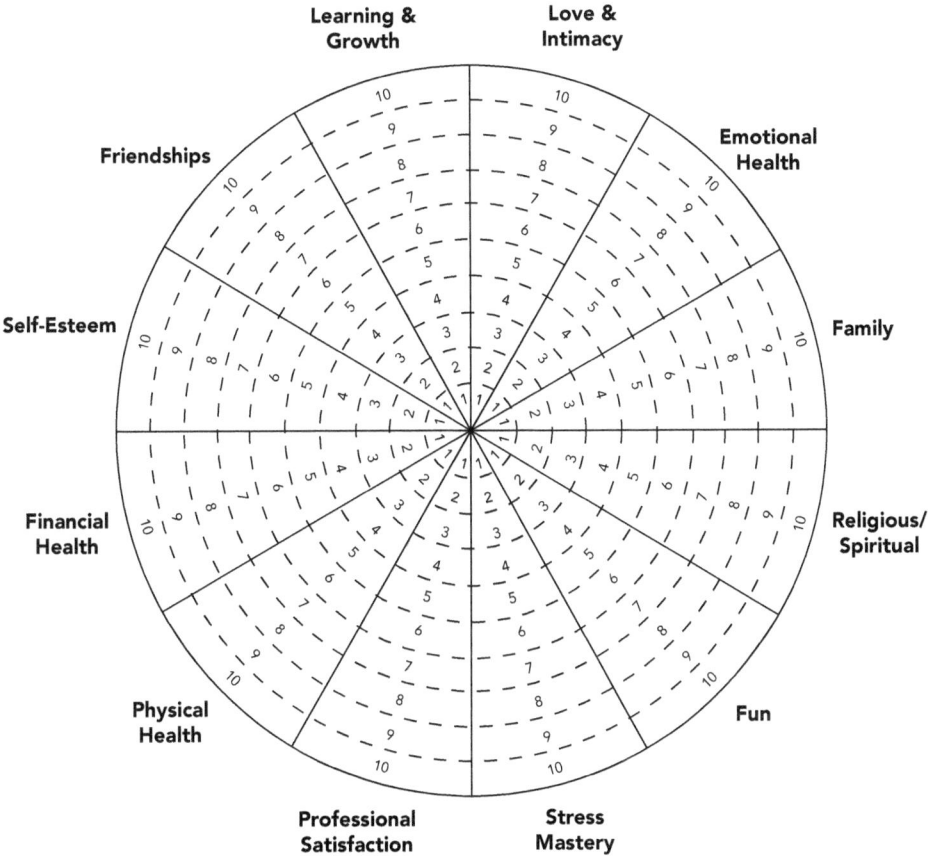

Shade in the rings or circle the number corresponding to the level of each experience in your life right now.

Focus on how you have felt in that given area in the last three months.

ASSESSMENT KEY	
0 = Completely lacking	6 = Adequate level in my life
1 = Close to nothing	7 = Content with what I have
2 = Very much lacking in my life	8 = More than content
3 = A little bit lacking	9 = Generous abundance
4 = Could be better, but getting by	10 = Are you kidding?
5 = Neutral; neither good nor bad	

automatic enrollment have a powerful influence on participant saving and investment behavior. Among new hires, participation rates more than double to 91 percent under automatic enrollment, compared with 42 percent under voluntary enrollment. Over time, eight in ten participants increase contribution rates, either automatically or on their own.

If retirement plan sponsors can use the inertia inherent in participant retirement-savings decisions to improve outcomes, why can't managers who coach do the same?

We're used to the idea that an organization is governed by principles, policies, cultural beliefs, and procedures that spell out how things work. But the idea that such laws or principles govern human nature raises the hair on the backs of many necks. Perhaps because of this, such laws have often been proposed with tongue in cheek—which makes it all the more disconcerting when they turn out to be backed by evidence. All managers who aspire to improve their coaching skills must be aware of certain principles of human nature, which play out in all organizations.

One example of a principle most managers are familiar with is the Peter Principle: in any organized environment people reach the level of their own incompetence. Economic and physics-based simulations have demonstrated this is more than just a cynical snipe at our bosses' knowledge, skills, and abilities.

Economist Edward Lazear postulated that every person's ability to do well on the job is determined by competence plus an additional transitory component determined by circumstance. There is no guarantee this transitory component will be maintained after a promotion, especially if the new position requires a different set of competencies. It is a view underpinned by simulations of promotion dynamics performed in early 2009 by physicist Alessandro Pluchino and colleagues at the University of Catania in Italy (*Physica A*, vol. 389, p. 467).

Dr. Pluchino discovered the Peter Principle would realistically act in any organization where the mechanism of promotion rewards the best members and where the mechanism at their new level in the hierarchical structure does not depend on the competence they had at the previous level, usually because the tasks of the levels are very different from each other. He was able to show, by means of agent-based simulations, that if the latter two features actually hold in a given model of an organization with a hierarchical structure, then not only is the Peter Principle unavoidable, but it also yields a significant reduction of the global efficiency of the organization.

What other laws or principles are most important for managers to understand and recognize, because they can derail the people you manage from their pursuit of mastery? Here are two that all managers aspiring to sharpen their coaching skills should become intimately familiar with:

1. Motivation Principle
2. Inner-game Principle

MOTIVATION PRINCIPLE

In the beginning of this book, I wrote:

> Self-interest is a strong motivator. When your team members believe *their* needs can be best satisfied by their work experiences, they will dedicate time and energy to achieve goals for you, their team, and the organization that makes it possible to fulfill those needs.

If someone can be motivated, it stands to reason they can also be demotivated. One foolproof way to ignite the spark of demotivation in the people you manage, and to halt their pursuit of mastery, is to ignore their needs or to subjugate them to the needs of your organization.

This is especially true when managing and coaching millennials, now the largest generation in the nation's history, supplanting the aging baby boomers. While I dislike generalizations about any group, there are some millennial characteristics all managers should consider. More than other generations before them, millennials

» Want to have impact. Millennials ask: "Am I making a difference in the world? Does my work matter?"
» Value collaboration.
» Trust technology over brand.
» Value experiences over other types of consumer choices.
» Often prefer their managers to be life coaches.
» Want their managers to be technology-savvy in enterprise/work options (e.g., project management tools like Asana) and social/play options (e.g., Snapchat Streak and Instagram Stories).

The first characteristic noted above might seem like a simple concept, but it's an important one. Yet very few managers understand how to seed and encourage feelings of purpose and meaning within individuals and teams. There are ways for managers to facilitate this sense of meaning and purpose. First consider what constitutes "meaning" at work—is it contributing to top- and bottom-line results? Is it having a positive impact on coworkers? Is it about making a difference in the community within which the organization operates? There are many ways to define meaning, and it's important for everyone who reports to you, directly or indirectly, to have clarity about what has meaning for them.

In addition to purpose, there are eight other basic needs that at different times motivate each of your team members, no matter what generation they are from. Fulfilling these needs can help build and strengthen the connections between their roles and the organization's purpose and helps each team member learn and grow.

The nine "Team-member Needs" section gives examples of how you as a coaching manager can tailor your approach and style to these different requirements.

Team-member Needs and How Managers Can Respond with Versatile Coaching Choices

Intellectual	Emotional	Psychological
Achievement	Purpose	Security
Focus	Autonomy	Belonging
Learning	Influence	Self-esteem

Intellectual

Achievement: When results, outcomes, and often material satisfactions are desired, the best managing style shows how performance and reward are linked; establishes clear goals and links them to rewards, especially financial ones when possible; and engages the competitive spirit with activity and competitions.

Focus: Desires knowledge, mastery, and specialization. The best managing style encourages setting ambitious targets, being a guide or mentor, and making introductions and connections with other experts to further increase expertise.

Learning: Desires training and development, innovation, creativity, and change. The best managing style involves idea generation and problem solving, recognizes creativity and innovation, and creates stimulating environments and safe spaces for brainstorming.

Emotional

Purpose: When finding meaning and making a difference are desired, the best managing style includes providing learning and significant project opportunities, connecting work with the larger picture of team and organizational goals, and giving feedback on making or not making a difference.

Autonomy: Desires freedom and independence. The best managing style includes sharing organization vision and goals, delegating responsibility, allowing autonomy, providing clarity about specific objectives, and creating clear boundaries.

Influence: Desires power and control over people and resources. The best managing style involves giving progressive responsibility and influence as they are earned, clarifying career prospects, identifying a mentor, and finding opportunities for stretching and expanding competencies.

Psychological

Security: When stability and predictability are desired, the best managing style involves establishing regular communication, clarifying roles, establishing routines and career paths, and creatively recognizing loyalty and service.

Belonging: Desires friendships and fulfilling relationships. Internally motivated when felt to be supported, consulted, and involved. The best managing style encourages a supportive and social work environment and has the manager regularly asking, "What do you think about this issue/challenge/opportunity?"

Self-esteem: Desires recognition and respect. The best managing style includes providing clear career progression and involvement in projects and consistently reviewing targets and goals. The manager understands the value of providing positive feedback—when deserved—to individuals with this need.

Is there any doubt when we feel more energized and perform better we believe one or more of these needs are being fulfilled? Whether it's Maslow's hierarchy or Hertzberg's motivation-hygiene theory, success and peace of mind are often determined by whether internal individual motivators are being met. For your team members, that's not necessarily entirely about money.

INNER-GAME PRINCIPLE

Team members' emotional and mental states—their *inner game*—have an impact on what gets done—the outer game. Managers tend to be hyperfocused on *what* is getting done. Results! Managers who also coach focus on results—"doing," as they should—but also on "being," as they must. Managing and coaching at this fifth and final rung must shift from a focus on helping people practice new behaviors in order to achieve goals and toward attention to and development of this inner game of beliefs and thoughts. To quote Gandhi:

> *Your beliefs become your thoughts,*
> *Your thoughts become your words,*
> *Your words become your actions,*
> *Your actions become your habits,*
> *Your habits become your values,*
> *Your values become your destiny.*

Managing and coaching have as much to do with helping people get out of their own way as with the mechanics of implementing action to reach a goal or target. Coaching calls on managers to pay attention both to the world around the people they manage and to the world within these individuals and teams.

All managers should aspire to build people's capacity to tune into and regulate internal emotional and mental states as they solidify new behaviors. This will help sustain the coaching behaviors leading to innovative breakthroughs in the outer game of achieving goals and targets. It will also strengthen your own coaching skills and abilities.

Brian Carlyle was someone I coached many years ago, and he desperately needed to get out of his own way. The inner game for him consisted of seemingly cemented beliefs about self-worth and the absolute value of his facts. This thinking colored his long presentations and reduced his ability to convey important information to his colleagues. In fact, it was becoming painful for his peers and team members to listen to Brian and appreciate his insights. Brian's inner and outer games were fomenting negative perceptions of him—with his boss, peers, and team members—which were diminishing his impact and influence.

When I first met Brian, he was the global marketing leader of a Fortune 500 public company. Brian's intelligence, knowledge of industry trends, and warm and engaging manner were on full display at our initial one-on-one meeting. It was clear to me—even on this first encounter—why he was one of the most published and respected marketing leaders in the industry.

Marketing professionals have a demanding role and must have many competencies. At the top of the list sits critical thinking: the ability to analyze massive amounts of data and complex market conditions and to determine their validity. This critical-thinking ability leads to creative thinking, which leads to solving business problems and finding and leveraging opportunities.

As I got to know Brian through our one-on-one coaching meetings, as well as through private, confidential meetings with his boss, peers, and direct reports, it was clear he excelled at a specific critical-thinking skill: the ability to employ multiple types of analysis to make sense of and render useful massive amounts of data.

Brian was an analytical thinker who could sift through vast amounts of data quickly and find valuable needles in haystacks for the myriad business units he consulted with. His insights about what this data revealed about consumer behavior and the efficacy of various marketing approaches were impressive to everyone who worked with him. He also knew how to look beyond the data and pick up on the trends and patterns that could lead to better, more successful marketing efforts.

There was, however, one need for improvement that emerged from everyone I talked with: meeting with Brian, while ultimately valuable, was a grueling and painfully long experience. Specific advice from the people he worked most closely with included:

» "Make people feel they are a part of the process and not just convinced that Brian has analyzed the process to death."
» "Make the main goal: consensus and increased dialogue."
» "Win over the crowd, win over the team. Too many people feel Brian is mainly interested in showing everyone he's right because he studied the numbers all day, instead of working toward consensus."
» "I know he knows a lot, but doesn't my opinion count for anything?"

The perception that Brian overanalyzed, was obsessed with his own set of facts and viewpoints, and didn't consider his audience in meetings and presentations was severely limiting his ability to bring people together to solve issues and implement marketing strategies. Even when he was right about something, people dreaded working with him.

As I shared this 360-feedback report with Brian, I discovered he was completely locked in to the following beliefs:

» He, and he alone, was the one who knew the most about any given issue, problem, or trend he was researching or analyzing.
» Data led to facts, and facts were inarguable. He prided himself on building bulletproof cases for every conclusion reached and strategy advanced, and he believed everyone should come to see this (AKA "his") irrefutable logic.

I recognized these beliefs as potential roadblocks to sustaining any behavioral changes Brian might decide to pursue with respect to goal setting and action planning. But it was too early in my coaching relationship with Brian to attempt to explore, let alone challenge, these rock-solid beliefs, which were part of his inner game.

Instead, I focused Brian's attention on hearing the 360 feedback, summarizing what he learned, and determining his interest in establishing a few developmental goals he could agree to work on for the next six months. He told me he was fully committed to making changes and agreed to establish and pursue some goals with my help.

Over the next four months, we made great progress. Brian was working diligently on two goals requiring three new kinds of behavior from him:

1. Involving people in helping shape the decisions that would affect them
2. Working collaboratively to arrive at conclusions
3. Saying more with less

Brian's boss gave him authentically positive feedback on the strides he was making. People took me aside to say how much better his meetings were: they were shorter; more to the point; and allowed for constructive discussion, feedback, and disagreements.

One of the early tools I shared with Brian involved altering his words when sharing his opinion. Traditionally, if someone said something Brian disagreed with, his words, tone of voice, and body language suggested he was not open to this other viewpoint. I suggested softening his approach more often by beginning a sentence with: "Here's how it occurs to me…" In this way, he was signaling to an individual or audience he did have an opinion; it might be a differing opinion, but he was potentially open to hearing something else too.

Brian and I had made good progress with *Disciplines 2, 3, and 4—Know Yourself, Align Destination, and Take Action*—but the hard part lay ahead. Could he sustain this behavior after the structure of our regular coaching meetings was removed?

Fortunately, I was now close enough to Brian to help him with his inner game. My hunch about his analytic bent, his predilection for placing his set of facts above all others, and his "irrefutable" logic had been confirmed by getting to know him and reviewing the results of two assessment instruments (MBTI® and FIRO-B®) I had asked him to complete during *Discipline 2: Know Yourself.* These two instruments also provided quantitative data—lots of it. As you can imagine, Brian dived in and made sense of it very quickly.

When it came time for our final structured meeting as coach and client, I took him to lunch at a waterfront restaurant in Laguna Beach, California. A friend of mine was a manager there. Before we arrived, I called her and made a reservation. I warned her I was going to make some strange requests and was hoping she could help me. She replied she would do her best.

I then requested a table for three, with three place settings, facing the ocean. I asked my manager friend if she would seat us, hand us menus, sit down with us, and launch into her two personal favorite dishes in the most excruciating, detail-oriented, long-winded, annoying, and logical way she could. "Your goal," I remember saying to her, "will be to convince us these are the two best things on the menu. And the only things worth ordering. Period."

I remember asking her to drone on until interrupted by my guest. However, the two dishes really had to be her favorites. I wanted her ultimate goal to be to get both of us to decide on one or both of those favorite dishes. She agreed to everything, and I closed the call with these admonishments:

» You and you alone know the most about the food choices you are recommending.
» Your knowledge and taste are inarguable; you pride yourself on these recommendations and want everyone to see that these two items are the best choices.

Let me pause my story briefly. In my experience as a manager and coach, there are three effective ways to get someone's full attention before sending an important message—a message you want never to be forgotten. One, use humor. Two, do something legendary and symbolic. And three, combine humor with something legendary and symbolic. With this upcoming lunch with Brian, I was aiming for #2 and hoping for #3. The best thing about these three methods is they don't have to cost a lot of money. You can touch someone very deeply and get your message across without spending much by going out of your way to do something special—to create something personal meant only for them that they won't ever forget. The best managers and coaches I ever had did this frequently.

Brian and I were escorted to our lunch table by my friend, who promptly joined us at the table and launched into her two favorite dishes. She wouldn't stop until finally Brian said, in a friendly but firm, and perhaps slightly pleading, tone, "Enough, please. Thank you. We understand these are your favorites, and we would now like to look at the menu and tell you what we want." The manager left and Brian looked at me, a little shell-shocked by her behavior.

"Brian," I said, "she does know a lot about the menu. She told us which items get the most attention from the chef. The high quality of ingredients used in her favorite dishes, where they do their sourcing, and…"

"All right. All right. You sound just like her," he said. "Let me take a look at the choices and give my opinion on this. I might have an opinion too, you know."

Wow, I thought. Right on cue. I pulled out a piece of paper, a page from his 360-feedback report with all the comments from people he worked with, and handed it to Brian.

I took out a red Sharpie from my coat pocket and circled the last quote: "I know he knows a lot, but doesn't my opinion count for anything?" My restaurant manager friend was walking back to the table as Brian stared at the page. She smiled at both of us, and he started laughing. It was the deep, closed-mouth laugh that sometimes happens when you're laughing at yourself.

I said, "Look out at the ocean, Brian. Those waves can never stop. They will be hitting that beach for thousands, maybe millions more years. But you *can* stop thinking that you, and you alone, have the definitive marketing answers at work. You can stop thinking everyone has to bow down to your bulletproof analyses. You've put this attitude aside for the last four months or so, and you've seen how people are reacting to a 'new you.' You will never master this completely. You will never be able to completely block out your inclination to 'be the expert.' That's all right as long as you keep up the pursuit. Remember this moment. Remember what you have practiced. Don't be like the ocean, doomed to repeat the same motions day after day after day."

Brian smiled, looked out at the ocean, and finally told our server what he wanted for lunch.

We imagine that we've traveled far from the inner-game thoughts and habits we left behind when, in reality, the wrong track is always running alongside us. Before we know it, we can be back doing things we swore we never would repeat and wondering how we got so lost again.

As the old adage goes, "You pick up where you left off." Unless…you have a manager you trust as a coach, who knows you and knows how to gently and relentlessly guide and nudge you back to the desired track and pursuit.

You can be that manager and that coach.

DISCIPLINE 5 SUMMARY

There is an inner sense in most managers I have met that constant mastery of something—anything—is actually unattainable. Those who earn the "master" brand or reputation are really just farther along the path, more advanced in their adventures, successes, failures, and skills than what we commonly observe. The diligent, persistent, and active *pursuit* of mastery is what you are after, not the achievement of mastery itself.

Managing and coaching have as much to do with helping people get out of their own way as with the mechanics of implementing action to reach a goal or target. Coaching calls on managers to pay attention both to the world around the people they manage and to the world within these individuals and teams.

All managers should aspire to build people's capacity to tune into and regulate internal emotional and mental states as they solidify new behaviors. This will help sustain the behaviors leading to innovative breakthroughs in the outer game of achieving goals and targets. It will also strengthen your own coaching skills and abilities.

ENERGIZERS

Here are some reinforcing and energizing ideas to consider when practicing Discipline 5: Pursue Mastery.

If you want someone to sustain new behaviors...

✅ Make it about the pursuit.

Research indicates 10,000 hours of practice are required to achieve the level of mastery associated with being a world-class expert in anything. In countless studies of composers, basketball players, concert pianists, chess players, and many other professionals, 10,000 hours comes up again and again. But remember this: 10,000 hours is not the goal. Perfection is not the goal. The active pursuit of mastery is the goal, while learning and improving are the by-products that keep on giving...to the people you manage and coach, to your organization, and to you.

✅ Focus on making other lives significant and worthwhile.

Create an additional personal goal this year that isn't just about achievement or an end result. Craft the goal by focusing on those things that make the lives of the people and teams reporting to you more significant and worthwhile. If achievements and accomplishments happen, great. But if they fall short, take comfort in knowing that you have enriched their lives in some way and will be contributing to the organization you work for in a very important way.

✅ Set upon the pursuit of giving rather than taking.

The pursuit of meaning is, in large part, what makes all of us uniquely human. For one day, one week, or one month, devote yourself to setting aside any selfish, self-centered interests and simply set upon the pursuit of giving rather than taking. Be even more generous with your time, energy, and focus for the team(s) you lead.

*"Unless you know what it is, I ain't never going
to be able to explain it to you."*
—Louis Armstrong

*"Treat people as if they were what they ought to be, and
you help them to become what they are capable of being."*
—Goethe

*"Everything can be taken from a man but one thing.
The last of the human freedoms—to choose one's attitude in
any given set of circumstances, to choose one's own way."*
—Viktor Frankl

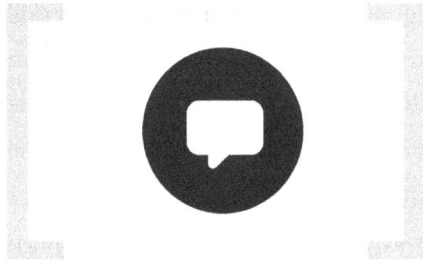

CONCLUDING COMMENTS

I end as I began. As a manager, you can put your coaching skills to work every day, helping your team members learn and grow as they participate in work that is meaningful…to *them*. Whether they are resolving customer issues, working on completing financial transactions, or bringing a new product to market, progress on what is important to them can make all the difference in their energy levels, commitment, and performance. The more frequently the people and teams reporting to you experience this, the more likely they are to be energized, innovative, productive, and aligned with you and their department, division, and company goals.

Managing *and* coaching is an accomplishment no less worthy than bringing in new business, reducing cycle times, or creating customers for life. It involves self-discipline, practice, and *shoshin* (having a beginner's mind). The route to its attainment produces positive and sustainable energy and results for the people reporting to you and for your organization.

Throughout this book, one of the major themes is that coaching complements and strengthens your management accountabilities. This rare combination of great management and great coaching skills and abilities is what creates legendary performance for your company and from your teams.

The business challenges today, and on the horizon, demand an urgent response: improve your coaching knowledge, skills, and abilities. Coaching is a competency that contributes to a high-performance culture and demands no less proficiency than setting strategy, developing budgets, interpreting financial and operational reports to make them actionable, and predicting or responding to market opportunities.

By focusing on the guiding principles and framework presented in this book, you will be able to sustain managing and coaching success over the long term. The *Coaching Ladder to High Performance* is purposely not academic jargon. It was not hatched from some mountain-top lab filled with thought leaders. It provides simple and practical ideas that can easily be applied to all managers who also want to coach.

What bedrock coaching principles and values do I consciously pass on to managers I meet and work with? Integrity is not negotiable. Learning never ends. The relentless pursuit of improving someone else's life—at work or home—is never guaranteed but always worth the effort.

Strengthening your coaching abilities will not occur on a straight road. There will be twists, U-turns, and unexpected potholes along the way, but they're nothing you can't handle now that you know the Five Disciplines of the *Coaching Ladder to High Performance*, which you can climb at your own pace.

There is an urgent need for managers to inspire and help deliver higher individual and team performance. We are talking about nothing less than revolutionizing the potential for organizational success. Organizations will change as managers learn to manage **and** coach. This makes improving the coaching skills of all managers a critical task in every organization.

As you pursue ever-higher levels of coaching proficiency, keep the following coaching laws in mind:

RICHARD'S COACHING LAWS

1. Have concerns, not worries.
2. Have goals and standards, not expectations.
3. Seek influence, not power.
4. See traits, not flaws.
5. Life and business lessons can happen at any age.
6. Know the difference between running and growing a business. (Thanks to Jim Widner, Regional President, KB Home, for this one.)
7. Better to walk to success than to run to failure. (Thanks again to Jim Widner.)
8. Coaching can open the door to a second chance to make a first impression.
9. Human behavior is like a Dylan lyric. You don't have to understand it to be intrigued and inspired by it.
10. You become a legendary manager when you consistently manage and coach.

MY BACK PAGES

Why do I strive to manage *and* coach? Beyond the great results I've seen this combination produce and have shared in this book, here are the two backstories that help answer this question.

My first management role was as a logistics supervisor with a successful chain of beauty salons. I had worked in the central warehouse and distribution center (DC) for a few years before the promotion and was familiar with the operations, the people in the DC, and managers and associates in many of the salons. I was not, however, familiar with the practice and art of managing, supervising, or coaching.

My new boss handed me a couple of long articles by Peter Drucker and said, "Good luck." He was not a manager *and* coach. I saw him after that initial encounter only when things went occasionally south. He was let go after six months, and a new manager was brought in from the outside to replace him.

My new boss was Holly Scott, and she became the person I have done my best to model whenever I manage individuals and teams. Holly was

» Always quick to credit me and members of our team for success, and just as quick to take responsibility when something went wrong.
» A risk taker who loved experimenting and "stretching rubber bands" at work.

» An energizer who cared about my goals as much as she cared about the goals of the company.

» Trusting and trustworthy.

» Clear about targets and goals and how they aligned with the vision of the business.

» Interested in my development as a supervisor and, more importantly, as a human being.

» Unforgettable (yes, legendary).

This early experience taught me a great deal about the unbeatable positive impact of managing *and* coaching.

I think the "way-back" backstory of my interest in managing and coaching, though, started when I was even younger, with repeated viewings of a movie touching something deep within me: *Jim Thorpe: All-American.*

That movie gave me my first glimpse at the short distance separating triumph from tragedy. And it tapped into the broader human condition by linking the attainment of an elusive inner calm with the fulfillment of Thorpe's deepest personal dream: to be a coach.

The film was a perennial feature on TV's weekly "Million Dollar Movie," a brilliant piece of pre-DVR programming that aired the same movie on six consecutive days and then twice on Sunday.

I viewed the film on our family's Zenith and taped it on my dad's reel-to-reel recorder, so I could fall asleep listening to it or hear it during the days I was too sick to go to school. Before Bob Dylan lyrics would take up yottabytes of space in my brain, I had memorized the Jim Thorpe script and was running wild and free between Pacoima, California, orange trees and open fields, like Burt Lancaster in the movie.

This was the first movie that made me cry. I don't mean soft, one-at-a-time tears rolling down my cheeks; I mean rivers of rhythmic sobbing. I didn't cry when Jim angrily spewed cigarette smoke and self-loathing at his wife, or when that sweet woman who loved him slapped him repeatedly in the face to get him to quell his rage and look closely in the mirror. I didn't cry when his Olympic medals were stripped away and he slammed his fist into the trophy case, shattering the glass, as his inner demons of bitterness feasted on the moment, growling, "They can have 'em!" No, my tears started at the end of the movie, when Jim was driving a beat-up truck, and those eternal grapes-of-wrath blues are visible on his clothes and in his eyes.

The truck moves with the traffic as some boys play football in a nearby field with dirt and blowing weeds. The ball sails through the air, takes a few bad bounces, and lands under one of the truck's slowly rolling tires. A loud popping sound is heard, and the truck screeches to a stop. When the boys approach to retrieve the ball, they find it flat and ruined, and they shove it in Jim's face.

Some of the boys blame Jim and his truck, and their angry tone clearly stings him. He stares at them from the driver's seat—sad, dejected, and defeated. A police officer rolls up on a motorcycle and orders Jim to stop holding up traffic. Jim pleads, "But I ran over the kids' football." "I said move along," the officer snaps. Jim's huge weathered hands clutch the wheel, and the old truck keeps its appointment with the traffic.

With the opening of the next scene, my tears increased, because I knew what was coming. It is afternoon—a new day—and a bright sun shines on the same dusty playground and the same group of boys. Jim walks on the field toward the boys, a gift in hand: it's a new football. They are ecstatic and immediately get into formation. A hike and then an errant pass from a sloppy play sends the ball end over end on a short, erratic ride. "Wait a minute," calls Jim. "That's no way to play football."

Jim asks a few questions and listens, then demonstrates and teaches the boys a few techniques. Their eyes were riveted on him, and my throat tightened. The boys ask if he can help them win their big game, so they can all earn medals. Jim agrees to help if they focus on doing what it takes to win and not on the medals. As the boys run and the dust rises from the field, Jim watches, and his eyes sparkle. One of the boys calls out to him. The words are simple, direct, and delivered without irony: "Okay, coach."

They're the words Jim has waited an eternity to hear, the words that bring a metamorphosis and a calm, confident smile. They're the dream stuff, the ringing acknowledgment of a personal hope fulfilled, the climax of a life lived in the quiet desperation Thoreau described.

Thinking about those two words today, I like to remember the skinny and shy boy swimming in the deep emotions he found each time he watched that movie.

The movie portrays Thorpe in many ways as a hero denied. One of his major disappointments, and ultimately his greatest redemption, is related to his desire to coach: to help people achieve their goals and improve their skills.

Keeping this definition in mind—to selflessly improve the knowledge, skills, and abilities of people and teams—I believe coaching is a manager's obligation to uphold and an energizing gift to give.

ACKNOWLEDGMENTS

Thank You Isn't Nearly Enough

My coaching clients, for letting me into your professional lives and opening doors to my own learning and growth.

The Coaching Trinity: Joe Wert, Don Stapp, Sharon Hulbert

Joe, you are simply the greatest manager and coach I have ever known. Thank you for seeing all the potential and never letting me off the hook.

Don, for your constant support, laughter, advice, and brilliant and colorful language. You helped me more than you can imagine.

Sharon, for your insightful, honest, and direct feedback, which always made me think and made me a better person.

Rick Isaac, for the "every day and night talks" that haven't stopped since we met each other so long ago. I wouldn't be managing and coaching if it weren't for your influence. You are my brother in life for all time. I'm lucky to know you.

Jay Hieatt, for your friendship, legal advice, and full-on critiques that improved this book and brought it closer to fulfilling my vision. This book would still be on the proverbial drawing board without your constructive comments and ideas. And, most of all, thank you for saying "hi" to me in Mrs. Elam's student government class.

Stan Slap, for faith in me, trust in me, and changing forever my view of the employee culture, the manager culture, and the customer culture. Your genius and generosity shine for all of us who work with you. I'm proud to be on your team.

Nancy Crowley, for twenty-plus years of friendship, editorial and design guidance, and the contributions to this book and to all our client projects.

Brooke Letitchevski, for your design ideas and supreme editing skills.

Dr. Bruce Heller, for constant encouragement and inspiring me to form my own company. You are the coach's coach.

Bob Wolpert, for reading an early manuscript of this book and not holding back. Our joint book on innovation is waiting in the wings, my friend.

Mike Deblieux, for thirty-plus years of advice, insight, and help anytime I ask. You are an amazing energizer to me and your clients. Your integrity shines from an eternal lighthouse for all to see.

Chris Stehman, Charlene Miller, and all the great leaders and managers at Yamaha, for the tough-love feedback and decades of trust. Your feedback improved this book immensely, and I'm grateful to know you.

Tom Norton, Jim Widner, Sue Sorensen, and the fantastic executive leaders and management team at KB Home, for the responsive and caring feedback on the early manuscripts of this book. The energy, pride, caring service, and commitment you demonstrate to every one of your customers came through for me in all your feedback and advice.

Julie Tesser, for your attention to detail, perseverance, and those little things that always make the big difference to clients, me, and this book.

Sue Zeidler-Evans, for your courage, smiles, and love. You inspired all you touched. R.I.P.

Sherry Benjamins, for your wit, intelligence, grace, optimism, and enthusiastic support.

Julie Winkle Giulioni, for the consistent and excellent advice always demonstrated in your professional practice and in your book.

Dr. Jeremy Lurey, for your invaluable suggestions and enthusiasm for this book. Yesterday the coachee, today the coach.

Regina Miller, for your brilliance, SMARTS, honesty, and support. We must work together more often!

Judy Belk, it's an honor to know you, and I was thrilled to receive your detailed notes about making this book the best it can possibly be. While I was not able to make every change you suggested, you essentially laid the groundwork for my next book!

Keith Oldridge, thanks, mate, for letting me be a small part of your world as you and your team steered through multiple challenges to achieve exponential growth and customer loyalty. And thanks for that steak and conversation in Melbourne. Unforgettable, just like you.

Brian Anderson, for your impeccable timing and wisdom. You provided the right comments at the right time to improve the manuscript draft of this book. No surprise there. You always improve any work I show you.

Jim Finkelstein, for your creative vision, clear writing, and thinking about what was best for me during challenging times.

David Rodman, for your leadership, faith in me, and encouragement when I chose a new path.

Dr. Aaron Shaeffer, for introducing me to coaching and helping me learn the art and science of assessments.

The Weaving Influence PR team—special thanks to Becky Robinson, Christy Kirk, Lori Weidert, Mike Driehorst, and Christy Lynn Wilson.

Holly Scott, for being my first manager-and-coach role model. I miss you. R.I.P.

Saving the best for next-to-last: **Don "Coyote" Ehrler,** who first encouraged and inspired me to write and find my voice.

And to **Melody Gilsey, Barbara Rollins,** and the **Zaroff—Bossuk— Newburn family**…for your love.

THE LIBERTY CREW FOUNDATION
(thelibertycrew.org)

The Liberty Crew is a nonprofit organization dedicated to helping families and individuals understand and proactively deal with the disease of addiction. They take a proactive approach to addiction by shining a light on the common factors that might lead to addiction as well as possible interventions. They accomplish this through education programs in schools, media outreach, and community events. For more information or to donate to The Liberty Crew, please visit them online at thelibertycrew.org or at Facebook.com/thelibertycrew.

In memory of Joshua James Isaac, a portion of the profits from sales of this book will be donated to The Liberty Crew Foundation.

RECOMMENDED READING

Brown, Brené. *The Gifts of Imperfection: Let Go of Who You Think You're Supposed to Be and Embrace Who You Are.* Center City, MN: Hazelden, 2010.

Dyche, Jill. *The New IT: How Technology Leaders Are Enabling Business Strategy in the Digital Age.* New York: McGraw-Hill Education, 2015.

Goldsmith, Marshall, and Mark Reiter. *What Got You Here Won't Get You There: How Successful People Become Even More Successful.* New York: Hachette Books, 2007.

Heller, Bruce A., PhD. *The Prodigal Executive: How to Coach Executives Too Painful to Keep, Too Valuable to Fire.* New York: AuthorHouse, 2009.

Hsieh, Tony. *Delivering Happiness: A Path to Profits, Passion, and Purpose.* New York: Grand Central Publishing, 2013.

Jennings, Jason. *Think Big Act Small: How America's Best Performing Companies Keep the Start-up Spirit Alive.* New York: Penguin Group, 2012.

Kaye, Beverly, and Julie Winkle Guilioni. *Help Them Grow or Watch Them Go: Career Conversations Employees Want.* Oakland, CA: Berrett-Koehler Publishers, 2012.

Kaye, Beverly, and Sharon Jordan-Evans. *Love 'Em or Lose 'Em: Getting Good People to Stay.* Oakland, CA: Berrett-Koehler Publishers, 2014.

Maister, David H., Charles H. Green, and Robert M. Galford. *The Trusted Advisor.* New York: Free Press, 2000.

Maxwell, John. *Good Leaders Ask Great Questions: Your Foundation for Successful Leadership.* New York: Center Street, 2014.

McChesney, Chris, Sean Covey, and Jim Huling. *The 4 Disciplines of Execution: Achieving Your Wildly Important Goals.* New York: Free Press, 2016.

Perkins, Dennis N.T., Margaret P. Holtman, Paul R. Kessler, and Catherine McCarthy. *Leading at the Edge: Leadership Lessons from the Extraordinary Saga of Shackleton's Antarctic Expedition.* New York: AMACOM, 2000.

Pink, Daniel. *Drive: The Surprising Truth About What Motivates Us.* New York: Riverhead Books, 2011.

Prager, Dennis. *Happiness Is a Serious Problem: A Human Nature Repair Manual.* New York: William Morrow Paperbacks, 1998.

Rath, Tom. *StrengthsFinder 2.0.* New York: Gallup Press, 2007.

Sandberg, Sheryl. *Lean In: Women, Work, and the Will to Lead.* New York: Knopf, 2013.

Sinek, Simon. *Start with Why: How Great Leaders Inspire Everyone to Take Action.* New York: Portfolio, 2011.

Slap, Stan. *Bury My Heart at Conference Room B: The Unbeatable Impact of Truly Committed Managers.* New York: Portfolio Hardcover, 2010.

Slap, Stan. *Under the Hood: Fire Up and Fine-tune Your Employee Culture.* New York: Penguin Publishing Group, 2015.

Williams, Pat. *How to Be Like Coach Wooden: Life Lessons from Basketball's Greatest Leader.* Deerfield Beach, FL: Health Communications (HCI), 2006.

ABOUT THE AUTHOR

Richard A. Greenberg is president of The BreakThru Alliance, an international coaching and consulting firm he founded in 2008, based in Marina del Rey, California. His innovative thinking has led to improvement in organizations ranging (alphabetically) from Avery Dennison to Yamaha Motor Corporation, and in size from small to very large. He is a former educator at USC's Marshall School of Business; was a principal at a "big six" accounting, tax, and consulting firm; has completed projects in more than thirty countries; served as chief HR officer for a media and entertainment company; and was operations manager at a successful retail chain. The BreakThru Alliance analytics and survey division was sold to The SLAP Company in 2014, and Richard continues doing coaching and culture survey work with SLAP consulting. He has published a dozen articles in business journals. This is his first book.

Richard lives in Los Angeles, California, with his wife of thirty-two years and has a grown son and daughter, who have taught him as many life lessons as he has hopefully taught them.

More information can be found at www.thebreakthrualliance.com, or you can email Richard at rgreenberg@thebreakthrualliance.com.

www.ingramcontent.com/pod-product-compliance
Lightning Source LLC
Chambersburg PA
CBHW062010200326
41519CB00017B/4747